MW01620653

COMING OUT BY GOING IN

THE FREEDOM TO BE YOURSELF

CASE ERICKSON

Library of Congress Control Number: 2019913275

ISBN: 9780578567419
E-Book ISBN: 9780578567457

Blue Buddha House
PO Box 381
Buda, TX 78610

CONTENTS

There are just too many people to thank for getting this piece of work out into the world! My mother, my father (who actually passed during the writing), my children, their mother, and my extended family and friends. I would not have had these amazing stories and be who I am without you. Thank you, thank you, thank you!

PREFACE

THE BEGINNING & THE END

Leave it to the universe to bring me inner peace at a big Baptist church in the middle of Texas.

It's probably because there was no pastor, and I was there at night in the middle of the week.

More than likely though it was the irony of divine timing.

It was a Thursday evening in the fall of 2017.

An Italian opera song was being sung by a choir of 6th graders, of which my son was a part.

As I sat in my pew, despite the propensity to be triggered by the religious PTSD from my surroundings, I was flooded with warmth, peace, and love.

Something greater than an altar call was at work.

See, a lot was "wrong" with my life at the time, yet I found myself completely in love with the moment in front of me as one particular face looked and sang back to me.

My son...my angel.

Singing a song with the other fairies in disguise, with lyrics in a foreign language that I still seemed to understand.

Joy.

As I sat there watching him as the perfect combination of his mother and me, I was flooded with the contrast and beauty of the masculine and the feminine.

I was also reminded of his younger sister (my amazing daughter), and I really felt, “Wow, I have it all.”

Thoughts flooded my mind. “Even though I don’t own a home, I have it all. Even though I don’t have a ton of money in the bank, I have it all. Even though I’m not living my ‘dream life,’ I have it all.”

And in that moment, I made my LIFE enough.

I made my health enough.

I made my bank account enough.

And I made that moment, made my children, enough.

My son…my daughter.

Enough.

It was all perfect.

Everything I did and didn’t do.

Perfect…

My time in the closet. My time out of the closet.

The masculinity and femininity within me — within us all.

All my heartache hating myself had led me to love it all right there in that moment.

Perfectly, enough.

Growing up under the religious dogma that programmed me with beliefs such as, "I'm not good enough, there's something wrong with me, I'm fundamentally flawed, and what I want is bad," all still somehow led me to this gorgeous moment at my son's concert that was held in a Baptist church.

Sitting in a symbol of the institution that laid the foundation for some of the most traumatic years of my life became the place where I found true love and what I believe to be our greater truth, beyond any religion.

That we ARE good enough.

There is NOTHING wrong with us.

We are fundamentally FLAWLESS.

And what we want is GOOD.

Everything is a gift.

And it's all Love.

I started tearing up in the middle of his song as the contrast and clarity flooded my soul.

We're here for the journey.

The adventure.

The ups, downs, and everything in between.

We're really just surfing waves and riding rainbows.

It hurts, and it's also f*cking fantastical (PS, pardon my occasional verbal zest).

Because who we are — the peace that passes all understanding — is right there in the middle of it all.

We, the observer, float along the center, observing the magnificent pendulum of the yin and the yang, and THIS is our Heaven within.

In each and every moment, we come out.

We go in.

And peace is found in the in between.

Being our true selves is the foundation.

That means that our lesson in life is to bring love and authenticity to all of it and express ourselves fully as such.

Before I knew it, the choir performance was over.

As I left the auditorium with my son, I knew in my heart that no matter what it took, I was going to share even more of myself and the lessons I have learned by living my authentic self.

I knew it was good...it was bad...and it was definitely ugly.

But more than anything, I knew I had to share it.

As we got into the car, I told my son I loved him, and he told me he loved me back.

I felt complete.

And the end...

Was just beginning.

INTRODUCTION

The twenty-four stories that follow are from key areas in my life where I was pushed to express myself more fully by leaning into the world of authenticity in new and powerful ways.

Even writing this book I've dealt with internal conversations about being not good enough nor being "accomplished" enough to author anything.

But I am not writing this book, this book is writing me.

Because for those of us on the fringes playing the brave authenticity game, there will always be something for us to stick our neck out for and accomplish.

And what I've learned about coming out of the closet is that ALL of us have fears and stories that can KEEP us there, and we ALL have closets to come out of.

Just being our authentic selves in and of itself is an act of bravery.

So this is my journey out of shame, fear, sadness, bitterness, anger, and resentment, into a space of happiness, peace, joy, forgiveness, and love.

Each story illustrates what I call the gift of contrast, and understanding this gift brings us OUT of shame and INTO love, no matter what "closet" of fear or limiting belief holds us back.

If you're looking for a way to bring more peace and power into your life, reconcile your relationships with any number of people in your life (including God), and if you're willing to do the work of being bravely, unapologetically, and courageously you, this book will challenge your ideas and push you out of your comfort zone into the freedom of your full self expression.

You will have access to a new zone of love and acceptance of all things within yourself, as you release resistance to people, places, and things that keep you in closets of fear and limited self-expression. You will have an increased love and appreciation for the joy of authenticity, as you live each day as the gift that it is.

I include exercises/applications to bring you back to what I call our "Sacred Orientation," which is the deep-down divinity that comes from knowing and aligning to the truth of who you are. You will be reminded that you are the observer of that pendulum, rather than the swinging weight.

You can complete the reading and applications however you see fit; the intention is to make it simple yet effective, so you may want to take the time to process, depending on the level of shame and/or fear you are working through. It is repetitive at times on purpose. We're reprogramming some things and moving our lives into more of an inquiry -- constantly challenging our beliefs and creating new ones that empower us to create a life we love.

I have intentionally added extra space with the sentence line structure as well because I want you to feel the space within you, and to feel that it is an easy read to take one day at a time.

Thank you for joining me. I hope my story resonates with you, and you fall in love with your inner authenticity junkie just a little bit more.

And more than anything, I hope you know that you create a more beautiful, engaging, and ecstatic world...just by being you.

"IF YOU DO NOT CHANGE DIRECTION, YOU MAY END UP WHERE YOU ARE HEADING."

— Lao Tzu

CHAPTER 1

GOOD NEWS, BAD NEWS

I found out the night before my 9th birthday.

My father, a Lieutenant in the Marines at the time, was deployed overseas, so my mother, brother, and I were taking our summer vacation at my grandparent's home in southern Florida.

As I laid in the bed, not quite asleep, my mother appeared at the door.

In her early 30's at the time, not only was my mother beautiful, she was also a beacon of love to my brother and me.

Having come from a broken home herself, she made deliberate intention to make sure we both knew that she loved us, and all her motivation came from love.

And for whatever reason, tonight was the night I would find out the meaning of my existence, or so I thought.

She started with the bad news.

I was bound for hell.

But the good news was that there was also a way out!

She didn't phrase it like that of course, but her questions began to boggle my mind.

"Do you know that Jesus died for your sins?"

"Do you know we've all fallen short of the glory of God?"

"Do you know that hell is a place created for those who reject Christ?"

As a not-quite-nine-year-old, about the only thing I could think was, "I don't want to burn forever, so I better say this prayer to make sure I don't go to hell."

"Fire insurance" I called it later in life.

Also known as, fear, for fear's sake.

Let me be clear, my mother had the purest of intentions.

Given her history, she wanted to protect me and provide me with what comforted her.

Also, what parent in their right mind wants their child to burn in hell?

She was doing her duty as a mother, and I love her for it.

And in my world today, sitting at my kitchen island at the ripe old age of 42, I feel that we are all ALREADY forgiven.

We are not fundamentally flawed: We are perfect, whole, and complete.

We are not worthy of punishment. We are worthy of freedom.

And the only hell we create is in our own minds.

But on that warm summer night, I did what any normal child would do.

I wanted relief from my fear, so I prayed that prayer.

And I did what I needed to do to please my parents.

And so it went for years.

I'm pretty sure I "got saved" at every summer church camp in my teens. I just had to make sure I was heaven-worthy.

All of the time I spent sneaking pornography (and participating in the "shameful" act of self-pleasure) was surely cause for God to rethink his judgment on me and determine I probably really deserved to go to hell.

So just to be safe I uttered that prayer again, again and again, and to seal the deal I came forward at any and all of the altar calls that I could.

I got baptized twice as well, as if to say, "Yo God, I'm serious, please don't come get me!"

The shame and guilt for existing was compounded during puberty, as this was the time I also discovered my "same sex attraction."

If I wasn't going to hell before, I SURELY was going to hell now that I had crushes on the boys in my class.

And so, my existence continued through adulthood, including an inauthentic marriage to a woman because I didn't have the awareness that I could live otherwise.

A life of shame and sadness, feeling guilty to be me, until I was 35.

It was then that I began my journey into self-acceptance.

FULL self-acceptance.

Leaving behind my life of betrayal and doubt, I embarked on the road of trust and surrender.

Giving it ALL up.

Bit by bit.

Piece by piece.

Crumb by freaking crumb.

I did the work.

I DO the work.

Each day I author a new story, governed by the universal principles that allow a new way to be.

A way to be free.

A way to be love.

And a way to be alive.

Turns out that being saved from my fake religious life meant taking the biggest leap of faith I'd ever known.

A leap into the mystery of life.

The mystery of heaven; the gift of hell.

Who would have guessed that finding God took losing my religion.

GIFT 1:
EMBRACE HELL AS ACCESS TO HEAVEN

While what happens when we die is debatable, there is no argument that fighting and waging war inside ourselves creates our own hell right here and now. This includes the hell about your past, whatever it is. The good news is that your past does not exist unless you choose it in the present moment. The way out of the mental gerbil wheel is to embrace all the programming that you received as a gift of contrast. Resisting it as anything other than a gift will perpetuate your hell. Embracing it as a gift, inside the world of contrast (we know what we want because we experience what we don't want), is your access to heaven. In each and every moment, embracing ALL of us is our key to freedom.

APPLICATION

Ask yourself, were there times in your life when you were told or felt that you were fundamentally flawed? When you felt damned no matter what? This could be in a religious context, or it could have been some other person or instance where you began to think, "There's something wrong with me," or left you with the feeling of suffering for no reason other than your existence. You could have heard this first from any primary caregiver, or from some other person(s) in your life. Write down a list of people or instances where you adopted this idea or ideas. Start with the most recent and move your way back. Take time to feel.

How would your life go if you held on to those stories and ran this same program?

What do you see happening if you stopped and chose to rewrite a new story?

Write down new commitments and a new program that you are committed to running. Promise yourself to give yourself grace for the authoring process.

____

____

____

____

INSPIRED ACTION:

Take at least ONE new step toward acceptance as well as letting go by meditating for at least 10 minutes today. If you meditate regularly, make a commitment to increase your time. Go someplace quiet, ideally outside. Turn off all phones and set a timer. Complete 20 minutes or more if time allows. The more the better. Come back to your breath, meaning, really feel your intake and outtake. Imagine the air filling your lungs and spreading space throughout all the cells in your body. **EMBRACE the inhale as your acceptance of everything that has created your life up until this point.** As you exhale, feel the anxiety, stress, and any tension leaving your body. You will have thoughts. Allow yourself to think whatever you want to think. Acknowledge the thought, and picture it like a cloud, vanishing into vapor, each cloud being replaced by another, but accepting that you are not the clouds, you are the sky. Be still, and also know that you're always in motion, so everything is OK.

After you have completed the action, take three deep breaths and repeat this phrase:

I accept the sacred orientation that is my knowing deep down. I acknowledge that I am loved and supported by the forces governing my universe, and I am a conduit of this love and support for myself and for others. I choose to love myself fully, to accept my past as part of my divine journey, and to forgive, appreciate, and embrace all the people, places, and things in my life as my access to that divine love. I orient myself now to my truth, my power, and my love within, and I author my life in a co-creative way that serves my highest good as well as the highest good of all those around me, free from any and all fears or doubts. I am my most authentic self, and I express myself fully as such to create a life I love. And so, it is.

"SHAME CORRODES THE VERY PART OF US THAT BELIEVES WE ARE CAPABLE OF CHANGE."

— *Brené Brown*

CHAPTER 2

ARRANGED MARRIAGES OF SHAME

"Kids, we need to talk," my mom told us with the most somber and fearful face I had ever seen her make.

"What is going on?" my 12-year-old self thought with angst.

My fear almost immediately matched hers.

"They're totally getting a divorce," my child brain continued with its worst-case scenario.

I didn't even have time to converse with my brother either, then 16, before I found us both seated on the couch across from our parents.

Tears streamed down my mother's face.

Even my Marine father looked like he was about to cry.

"Oh sh*t, one of them is dying," I began to panic in my head, and at this point I hoped it was just divorce.

My mother began sobbing uncontrollably so my dad interjected, "There's something we need to tell you."

"NO KIDDING!" I thought to myself, now starting to get exasperated.

My father began, "Before your mother and I met, she had a relationship with another man, and they had a child."

"WAY TO GET RIGHT TO THE POINT DAD!" I think now as an adult.

Not barely twelve at the time though, I'm pretty sure my thought was something like, "What the actual f*ck?"

Shock? Not even an appropriate term.

Awe? Doesn't even begin to scratch the surface.

As children, we had grown up under strict Southern Baptist law.

My mother was a teacher at the Christian private school that my brother and I attended.

Combine that with a lieutenant colonel father, and we had lived under the premise of the "Biblical definition of marriage" as what was to be modeled for living.

But underneath that was a life of secrets and shame.

The thing about shame, particularly shame around sex and/or sexuality, is that we adopt the program so early in life.

We come out of the womb naked, and generally we have zero problem with exposure.

If you see a baby protesting, chances are it's because it's cold, wet, or experiencing some other level of discomfort.

It's not crying because it's thinking, "What is everyone thinking about my body?"

Yet somewhere along the line of our personal development we adopt the idea that covering ourselves is what is socially acceptable.

Nakedness becomes a "private" thing.

We learn what's appropriate, what the boundaries are between people, and what's acceptable along the lines of relating to our bodies and other humans.

Also stated, we get a sh*tload of information to process.

And if you grew up in a religious home like I did, the story was ABSTAIN, ABSTAIN, ABSTAIN from anything sexual.

Some of the programming I received included:

"Do NOT have sex before you're married."

"God's plan is one man for one woman."

"Homosexuality is an abomination."

"Sex creates a BOND FOR LIFE, so choose wisely."

"Save yourself and stay PURE for your wedding day."

And the list goes on and on.

Moral of the story: sex could be dirty, and it was certainly very serious business.

As a sexual human being, particularly one whose orientation was "less than straight," I was damned if I did, and damned if I didn't.

For my mother, she had fallen in love with her high school sweetheart (who was not my father), and when she found out she was pregnant, they were going to get married.

Around that time, her best girlfriend also got pregnant and married her sweetheart.

However, my mother was not so fortunate.

Her boyfriend ended up breaking up with her, and her mother sent her to an unwed mother's home, where she was not visited AT ALL, even though she was living just miles from her home.

Can you imagine being pregnant and not getting to share that experience with anyone you love?

For over six months, her mother and stepfather had told everyone that she was visiting her dad in Puerto Rico, and upon her return to "society," she was forced to transfer to a brand-new school in her senior year, as to avoid "excessive questioning."

And to add insult to injury, my mother had to care of her daughter for almost a week before giving her up for adoption.

Knowing my mom today as the big ball of love that she is, I can't imagine how hard that must have been for her.

When she got back home, she asked her mother if they were going to talk about the baby.

"What baby?" was her response.

My mother — now her mother's shame.

Shortly after mom graduated high school, she met my dad in a bar, and six weeks later they were engaged.

She wanted out of the house, and my dad was the way.

No romance. No real love. No connection.

But it was a way out of shame, or so she thought.

And so it went for twenty-something years until the daughter she gave up for adoption (my half-sister) ended up contacting her, thus triggering the conversation that my mom was having with my brother and me right there on that sofa.

I'm not sure if we would have ever known about my half-sister had she not reached out to connect with my mom; that's how deep the shame program was running.

It was literally a STORY of shame my mother was living under.

And it was unraveling.

As my story unravels for you now.

It's perfectly ironic that I was on the brink of puberty when I found out the "real truth" about my parents.

Everything about my family was changed in that moment.

Everything felt like a lie.

Because inauthenticity?

It never works.

It was about ten years after all this when I was in my early 20's when my parent's marriage would dissolve as a result of the inauthenticity of their original commitment.

Ironically/not ironically, I repeated it in my commitment to my fiancé around that time as well.

Without me being aware, I ended up making a commitment to inauthenticity.

Thinking, "Good boys don't have sex before marriage, and they certainly aren't gay," I married the first girl (or person for that matter) who I had ever slept with.

I didn't think I was gay. I thought I was straight, with a problem.

A problem that could be fixed.

I was going to MARRY MYSELF OUT of shame...just like my mamma!

Shame had arranged her marriage, and it ended up arranging mine as well.

But here is the deal about shame programming:

We will continue to run and write the patterns like computer code until we learn to undo them and transcend the grip that they have on us.

We literally recreate our parental story with our own adult relationships as a means to make them right.

In my marriage to a woman, I got to be both my father and mother.

Like my father, I was cold, distant, judgmental, disconnected, and controlling.

And like my mother, I was stoic yet tended to play the victim to my father's whims.

So I wanted to perfect my upbringing by manifesting a second version of it.

Yet beautifully, I perfected it not by staying in it, but by letting it all go.

See friend, I don't care what your orientation is, the way out of shame is not to run away from it.

It's to EXPOSE it.

To go in...

...And then to come out.

We can stop running and hiding, and just choose to stop trying to fix it all.

Quit our attempts to fix our mothers, our fathers, or ourselves.

There is nothing to fix.

Nothing to perfect.

Because it's already perfect.

All that it is, and all that it isn't.

In my world, being out with it all is the only way to live.

And that's the new program I get to write again and again.

That every.damn.day. is a gift.

A gift of acceptance, peace, and beautiful surrender.

In my hands each and every moment.

To be free from shame.

To be free from fear.

And to be all that we were created to be.

It was beautiful to see how my parents thrived apart from one another.

And even more beautiful is how my mother accepts me just as I am.

She broke the cycle of shame.

And now I'm breaking it too.

It starts with us.

It ends with us.

And somewhere in the middle...

There is Life.

The choice is yours; till death does YOU part.

GIFT 2:
EMBRACE SHAME AS ACCESS TO HONOR

The only way out of shame is to go through it. Resistance is futile. Fighting shame is still shame. Forgiveness starts with acceptance. And acceptance starts with forgiveness. Embrace your experience of shame as a gift of contrast to give you access to know what honor is. Honor your past. Honor yourself. Honor it all. And in that embrace, find your freedom.

APPLICATION

Ask yourself, was there a time when either you felt ashamed about something sexual, or you witnessed someone else being ashamed because of either having a child out of wedlock, having sex before marriage, or perhaps some other sexual trauma you experienced that caused you to think that there was something shameful about sex. Write down those people, places, or instances. It doesn't need to be lengthy. This is just for you to recognize and acknowledge when a story was implanted.

____

____

____

____

____

How would your life go if you held on to those stories and ran this same program?

____

____

____

____

____

What do you see happening if you stopped and chose to rewrite a new story?

____

____

____

____

____

Write down new commitments and a new program that you are committed to running. Promise yourself to give yourself grace for the authoring process.

____

____

____

____

INSPIRED ACTION:

Write down a list of all the things you feel ashamed of. This could be just a sentence or two, a paragraph, or pages. Let your darkness out. Give it room to express itself. EMBRACE IT. When you feel like you're finished, destroy the paper. The best way to do this is by burning it in some way (in a safe manner), or to rip it up and flush it down a toilet. Every time you feel shame over something about yourself or something in your past, remind yourself that you **transmuted the energy** of those thoughts and feelings. It all starts with allowing yourself to feel and process. The thoughts and feelings are not going to go away overnight and will possibly never go away, but your reaction to them can surely change. The point is for you to recognize that they are just thoughts — stories that keep you from being your fully-expressed self, and you have within you the power to transform them in an instant. Bringing the physical experience into being is an excellent tool to use as a reminder to burn/flush/transmute them again, again, and again. I also highly recommend the work of Byron Katie's, "Loving What Is" in transforming how we relate to our thoughts.

After you have completed the action, take three deep breaths and repeat this phrase:

I accept the sacred orientation that is my knowing deep down. I acknowledge that I am loved and supported by the forces governing my universe, and I am a conduit of this love and support for myself and for others. I choose to love myself fully, to accept my past as part of my divine journey, and to forgive, appreciate, and embrace all the people, places, and things in my life as my access to that divine love. I orient myself now to my truth, my power, and my love within, and I author my life in a co-creative way

that serves my highest good as well as the highest good of all those around me, free from any and all fears or doubts. I am my most authentic self, and I express myself fully as such to create a life I love. And so, it is.

"DON'T YOU EVER
LET A SOUL
IN THE WORLD
TELL YOU THAT
YOU CAN'T BE
EXACTLY WHO YOU ARE."

— *Lady Gaga*

CHAPTER 3

NEAR DEATH & NAKED

Everyone who says they have a near-death experience says that there is a warm glowing light at the end of the tunnel.

Everyone but me that is.

It was my last night as a 33-year old, which clearly warranted a heavy celebration.

I was running three restaurants at the time, I deserved a little break for God's sake, right?

Having two children, ages 4 and 1, a "break" usually meant drinking until I passed out after we put them to bed.

And tonight was no different.

Other than I did more than pass out.

I went unconscious.

But before I get to that, let me just say that running three restaurants had taken its toll.

Expanding from one to three units too quickly, mixed with the economy tanking, led to deep financial strain...enough to substantiate my use of an anti-anxiety/anti-depressant to be able to cope with the day to day drama of being in the food service industry.

It was not uncommon for me to partake in wine in addition to being medicated, but tonight was my birthday, which called for a departure into the land of tequila and homemade margaritas.

Even after consuming three of these though, I still felt fine.

It was not until I went to the cottage behind our home to visit our temporary guest that I got pushed over the edge.

I smelled it as soon as I walked in.

He was smoking marijuana out of some homemade coke can bong, and naturally offered me a hit shortly after I made my entrance.

After I thought, “Meh, why not, it’s my birthday,” I took a drag or two, completely oblivious to the fact that I probably looked like a total drug addict.

Turns out Prozac, margaritas, and weed do not play well together.

Who knew?

See, it wasn’t so much that I wanted to party; I wanted to check out.

Check out of my fake house.

My fake marriage.

My fake life.

I thought just a few hours break would suffice.

But that night on my 34th birthday, I got more than three hours.

I got a journey out of my body...and into the unknown.

And there was no freaking tunnel of light.

As I shuffled down the breezeway on my way back from smoking in the guest house, it hit me like a ton of bricks.

I collapsed almost instantly and began vomiting violently.

Shortly thereafter my wife showed up, and I realized I was also completely catatonic — able to hear everything around me, but unable to utter one coherent sound.

She was asking me questions, and all that came out of me were gurgles and moans.

I was terrified.

"Do you want me to call an ambulance for you?" she asked me as I was hurling my guts into the nearest toilet.

My thoughts were a mixture of, "Oh my God, this is how people who overdose must feel, is this the end, and YES call the damn paramedics," but all that came out of me was the heavy moan of a desperate, "Uuuuuuuggggghhhhhh."

And within a handful of minutes attempting to "wake me up" (to and including hosing me down in the shower), she was calling 911 and I was being loaded into an ambulance.

"Is he on medications?" yelled the paramedic.

"No" replied my wife.

"I think he's on Prozac!" chimed our guest from the shadows.

Apparently, my attempt at dealing with my depression was not so secret.

"Oh really?!" barked one of the EMT's. "Why didn't you tell us that? Has he ever tried to kill himself before?"

"No, no, no, he's just stressed with our restaurants," remarked my wife.

"Oh yeah? Which restaurants?"

"Main Street Wings."

"Oh yeah? We love Main Street Wings!"

At this point, I am completely mortified because the emergency personnel have identified me as someone in the community...someone who has more than likely waited on them at dinner.

My horror was further solidified when at this moment I started having a seizure.

"Mr. Erickson," said the EMT, "Since you're seizing, we're going to need to take a rectal temp. And we're going to cut and remove your clothing to do so."

GRRRRREEEAT, just what I had planned.

To get naked in front of my restaurant regulars.

Maybe it was this mortification that pushed me over the edge and out of my body, but regardless, it was at this point that I started my disconnection from the physical.

I started noticing a feeling of lightness — floating.

Conscious, yet feeling a complete lack of gravity.

Swirling around the ethers of the scene, it was like I was a part of everything, being relieved of my singular "Mr. Erickson" perspective.

Before long, my consciousness began to expand even further.

I felt as if I was leaving that ambulance.

Then I realized I WAS leaving that ambulance.

I was in the process of leaving my body behind.

"NO! NO! NO!" I quickly thought to myself or thought to somewhere.

"I CANNOT leave my family in this mess!"

I was gripped with fear.

No bright warm light.

No tunnel into everlasting love.

Just terror at what I had created and left for them.

And within an instant I was back.

Gravity and pain taking its toll, and the reality of my catatonic state sinking back in as well.

Before I knew it, I was being wheeled into our local hospital.

Cold and alone, comforted only by an elderly woman across the triage, staring at me with her gaping and equally sad mouth, I went through all the tests and rehydration treatments necessary for a temporary junkie such as myself.

And after hours of my toxic blood being rehabilitated back to “normal,” I was released.

Shortly after my painful taxi ride home, I collapsed on the bed, under a heap of covers, gratitude and remorse.

It wasn’t a deliberate choice to tempt the angel of death, but it would be the event that would start the domino effect of getting me out of my old life.

Out of my old house.

Out of my old marriage.

And out of my closet of shame.

Physical nakedness led the way to the exposure of my soul, revealing my truth, and finding my way.

And find my way I did.

GIFT 3:
EMBRACE WEAKNESS AS ACCESS TO STRENGTH

Scriptures say that in our weakness God is strong, and this is your gift right now. It's OK to have a weakness. We cannot all be strong in all areas of our life all of the time. It's an impossible standard of perfection that will inevitably leave us exhausted. In our willingness to admit that we have issues, we find great strength. Our independence is created by embracing our dependence on our own weakness AS WELL AS strength within ourselves.

APPLICATION

Ask yourself, are there areas in your life where you are self-medicating? This could be shopping, eating, gambling, online activities, social media, sex, drugs, or alcohol. The substance or activity is not the "problem," it's your dependence on it and the way in which you partake of it. You and only you know the point at which it turns into a common enjoyment of one cookie into devouring the whole box because you're attempting to deal with powerlessness, shame, or guilt over something in your life. What is that thing or things?

____

____

____

____

How would your life go if you held on to this way of being and continued your current course of actions?

____

____

____

____

What do you see happening if you chose to rewrite a new story?

____

____

____

____

INSPIRED ACTION:

Starting right now, commit to at least one full day of living a dependent-free existence. Who would you imagine the person to be who honored their health and their time? Close your eyes and imagine who they would be, then embody that person. Really get into a good game of pretend and allow yourself to feel it. Rather than thinking what you'll abstain from, think of what you will partake of. A walk outside instead of getting on social media? Reconnecting with your partner instead of sneaking pornography? Passing on the soda or cookies, instead of eating a whole box? Only you know what the best version of you would do, and today's action is about being that person RIGHT NOW, instead of having to have your whole life at a glance figured out.

I am neither a doctor nor a therapist, so if you are under the care of a doctor, please consult with them. I am not advocating quitting medications, I am advocating taking a baby step to be your future self, which may or may not include medication. Only you know where you are giving up your power, and this action is about being a more powerful version of yourself, if only for a day.

Depending on when you are reading this, it could be the rest of today or tomorrow. The point is, commit to just one day, and live it like the healthy, wealthy, and wise person you know deep down you are. You can worry about the next day after you live through this one.

After you have completed the action, take three deep breaths and repeat this phrase:

I accept the sacred orientation that is my knowing deep down. I acknowledge that I am loved and supported by the forces governing my universe, and I am a conduit of this love and support for myself and for others. I choose to love myself fully, to accept my past as part of my divine journey, and to forgive, appreciate, and embrace all the people, places, and things in my life as my access to that divine love. I orient myself now to my truth, my power, and my love within, and I author my life in a co-creative way that serves my highest good as well as the highest good of all those around me, free from any and all fears or doubts. I am my most authentic self, and I express myself fully as such to create a life I love. And so, it is.

"HOW WONDERFUL IT IS
THAT NOBODY NEED WAIT
A SINGLE MOMENT
BEFORE STARTING
TO IMPROVE
THE WORLD."

— Anne Frank

CHAPTER 4

CHRIST ON TV

"Touch the screen for healing!"

"Send me your money and God will bless you!"

"Father forgive me, for I have sinned..."

Those are just some of the things from my youth I remember hearing from televangelists.

But if Christ was alive today, do you think he'd be on TV?

I think he'd probably be cooking dinner for a friend.

Or maybe in the park talking to a stranger on a park bench.

Anyway, at this moment in time, he may as well have been on TV, because something divine definitely moved me that night as I accidentally overheard a televangelist.

I have been hit by bricks in the past, so I am extremely grateful that this was just a gentle nudge -- a whisper if you will -- that would set forth a string of events that would change the trajectory of my life forever.

It would spark the first domino that would mean me moving out of a home I had lived in for five years, out of a state I had lived in for almost twenty, and eventually out of a marriage I had been in for fourteen.

But back to God on TV...

I was making my bed with what I thought was an infomercial playing in the background.

Turns out it was a televangelist, and he must have been between his "prodigal son" and "send your money to the Lord" moments, because I kept it on the channel even though I wasn't really watching.

He was speaking of Peter's miraculous catch of the fish.

If you haven't heard of that passage, it's from John 21 and goes something like this:

Peter had been fishing all night long, but to no avail.

Then in the wee hours of the morning Christ appears on the shore of the lake and tells Peter to try the other side of the boat.

Peter obeys without hesitation and manages to catch so many huge fish (153 to be precise) that he cannot even bring the net in by himself.

The pastor was using this passage to display what he called, "The Law of Place."

He said, "You can be doing the right thing in the wrong place."

That struck a chord in me, and I stopped making the bed right then and there.

In the middle of fluffing the comforter, Spirit spoke to my heart.

"It's time for you to go. This is not your home," it whispered to me.

As crazy as that sounded to me, I didn't protest or resist.

It just felt right.

Insane, and right.

And when my wife felt the same way when I talked to her about it the next day, I knew it was our time to go.

We didn't even know where we were going, just that it needed to be a completely fresh, new start.

Turns out that it would be Austin, Texas.

About 1,600 miles away from our northern Virginia home.

No family.

No friends.

No jobs.

No "real" reason, other than both of us being desperate for change and thinking a drastic move would bring it about.

See, we had tried for SO LONG to fix our relationship.

New cars, new houses, better jobs, starting one restaurant, then adding two more, moving again, and in between all that having couples counseling, trial separations, ex-gay camps, reparative therapy, and any other book or church you can think of in the process.

Moving across the country was our last-ditch attempt to "fix" ourselves.

Before we left, I remember saying, "I'm not in love with you, but I love you."

And then her agreeing, "Yeah, me too."

Sounds like the perfect recipe for a happy marriage, yes? (insert sarcasm here).

Needless to say, we were in Austin for less than six months when we were out of money, out of work, and WAY out of love.

Turns out that Jesus on TV didn't need me to get to Austin so much as he needed me to just go.

To cast my net on the other side of the boat one last time and see just what would happen.

To take that leap.

We weren't in love with each other, and deep down we both wanted something better for our lives.

Turns out, that something better would be the end of "us," and the beginning of me.

The ground zero reboot.

Within six months I experienced bankruptcy, foreclosure, and divorce, and would come out of my final closet of shame.

Not quite the abundance I'd planned/hoped for, and in hindsight I'd pay any price to experience again.

That is the gift of getting to nothing.

Turns out that nothing really is everything.

A journey to God that would feel like the end, yet also one that's been beyond the beginning.

GIFT 4: EMBRACE INSECURITY AS ACCESS TO SECURITY

This story is one part taking the leap in my relationship with my spouse and one part taking a leap in my relationship with God. Keep in mind that at the time I did not relate to myself as gay, just straight with a problem. And moving across the country was just the latest of attempts to fix what was impossible to fix. But at the time it felt like the right thing to do, as opposed to staying stagnant. It was scary to move to a town where we knew no one, and where neither of us was employed, but that drive to leap was stronger than anything else.

Things certainly did not go the way we thought they would, and leaps rarely do. But it's hard for me to imagine what would be occurring right now if we did not take that leap, so there's just no way I'd live life any other way than to follow that still small voice of semi-insanity, so that's what I'm going to ask you to do right now.

There is wisdom in insecurity — knowing that you don't know — and being OK with the process, is where the joy of surrender is born.

Now is the time to leap.

APPLICATION

Ask yourself, are there areas in your life where you are holding on to a belief that says you can't or shouldn't do, say, or be something? If so, what are they?

____

____

____

____

____

How would your life go if you held on to this way of being and continued your current course of actions?

____

____

____

____

What do you see happening if you chose to rewrite a new story?

____

____

____

____

INSPIRED ACTION:

I am not advocating for you to quit your job, unless you feel strongly that's what you are to do. Only YOU can answer what is right for you to do. But if there is something you've been putting off doing — it could be as simple as telling someone how you feel about them — now is the time to do it. Decide what you're going to do and make a commitment to do it in a timeframe that feels semi-scary to take. It really depends on what your leap is. There are whole books on how to leave a job/create a business, so this lesson today is more about doing one thing that pushes you out of your comfort zone, even if it's telling a family member you love them or you're sorry for something, getting uncomfortable is the way we grow. So, take the leap, and see where and how you land.

After you have completed the action, take three deep breaths and repeat this phrase:

I accept the sacred orientation that is my knowing deep down. I acknowledge that I am loved and supported by the forces governing my universe, and I am a conduit of this love and support for myself and for others. I choose to love myself fully, to accept my past as part of my divine journey, and to forgive, appreciate, and embrace all the people, places, and things in my life as my access to that divine love. I orient myself now to my truth, my power, and my love within, and I author my life in a co-creative way that serves my highest good as well as the highest good of all those around me, free from any and all fears or doubts. I am my most authentic self, and I express myself fully as such to create a life I love. And so, it is.

"BE YOURSELF. EVERYONE ELSE IS ALREADY TAKEN."

— *Anonymous*

CHAPTER 5

JESUS & SUICIDE

Just because I said I lost my religion, you may think that I am anti-Christian, which I am not.

In fact, it was a story about the man named Jesus that saved me from the state of hopelessness I found myself in after being married for almost 14 years.

It was just before Christmas in 2011.

I had my bottle of Benadryl and a liter of vodka, and I was so utterly done with my life that I was finally willing to see what would happen.

I was in a personal development course at the time, and the basis of one of their homework assignments for me to think about was that I was, "Perfect, whole, and complete."

I thought to myself, "If I am perfect, who needs God?"

This of course sent me into the biggest crisis of faith...to which my sexual orientation was always the center of.

For years it had been my cross to bear.

The thorn in my flesh...

My shadow...

My demon...

My sadness.

But before I swigged that cocktail on that chilly winter night, something in me/around me/beside me wasn't totally convinced it was my time.

A thought occurred to me: "Let me just pretend I don't know ANYTHING about God.

Let me entertain the idea that everything that anyone has ever told me could be wrong.

Let me forget about all the other 'Bible' verses, and just start with some Jesus.

I had heard the book of John was good for that, so I opened up the Bible to see what "randomly" popped out to me.

And that night I was led to the story of his healing of the cripple at the pool of Bethesda.

Two things stood out to me about this passage:

Not only did Christ heal the cripple, but he told him to take up his mat and walk.

Did you know that the acts of healing as well as carrying something were against the law on the sabbath?

My boy was a LAWBREAKER!

At the time I thought that the Bible said that being gay was a sin (to which I

now know is not true), and it was in this moment that I understood more of who Christ was.

It didn't matter if it said being gay was a sin or not, whoever God was, they wanted me to be free MORE THAN what I perceived the law to be at the time.

"God" wanted me to live my TRUTH more than they wanted me to live a lie.

See, up until then I felt like I was a straight guy with a problem.

But that night I was set free.

And for the first time in my 35 years I felt OK to be gay.

Then I thought, "If it's OK to be gay, why am I married to a woman?"

Oh, the irony.

See friend, in my opinion, sin is nothing more than believing the illusion that we are separated from Love.

And I was hating myself.

My marriage to a woman, while there was some love present, was rooted in hate of self.

And that life in the closet?

THAT...was living in sin.

Hating MYSELF was missing the mark of divine connection way more than LOVING someone of my same gender ever could.

And now?

The past 7 years have been some of the most incredibly challenging as well as rewarding times of my life.

Loves gained.

Loves lost.

Business successes.

Business failures.

Single parenthood drama.

Fatherhood miracles.

Bumps, bruises, hugs, and love.

ALL of the things of beauty and chaos.

Are there dark days?

Of course.

Does “my demon” show its face from time to time?

Abso-freakin’-lutely.

But you know what?

The ONLY one who made that closet was me -- by believing a lie.

And I am the ONLY one who will choose TRUTH every. damn. day.

I am the light.

You are the light.

WE are the light.

WE (gay, straight, or anyone in between) are THE ones who can bust down the walls of ALL closets, so that all of humanity can be free.

By living our courage.

By being fully ourselves.

And being One with the Spirit of all things.

I am eternally grateful that I didn't off myself all those years ago, and it's my prayer that not one person nor one religion lead anyone to live a life of hate.

Deep down I feel we'll make it...one rainbow at a time.

GIFT 5:
EMBRACE THE LAW AS ACCESS TO THE SPIRIT

As much as I want to hate the black and white legalistic mentality of much of the Bible (particularly the old testament), I am not moving into the space of love that Christ was by staying in the hatred of it. He came as an embodiment of God — spirit incarnate — to show us what

Love could do. Which is so much more powerful than any law. Regardless of your thoughts on old testament writings/Christianity on the whole, the point I want to make is that the joy of the spirit is made known now because we previously lived under an old image (law) of God.

A land of rules, doctrine, and dogma can now be replaced by the rapturous world of freedom, healing, and mystery, but it is up to us to believe that it's possible. That there is an energy that is FOR us (spirit), rather than against us (law). If you're struggling with rationalizing dogmatic theology, I highly recommend the book, "The Universal Christ," by Richard Rohr.

APPLICATION

Ask yourself, are there areas in your life where you are holding on to a belief that says you have to follow certain rules in order to be accepted? If so, what are they?

___

___

___

___

___

___

___

How would your life go if you held on to this way of being and continued your current course of actions?

What do you see happening if you chose to rewrite a new story?

INSPIRED ACTION:

Take out a piece of paper and draw a vertical line down the middle to separate it into left and right sides. On one side write, “Old Law,” and on the other side write, “New Spirit.” Take time to reflect on the old rules or labels you have been given. And on the right side of them write a new commitment or way of being that could bring you more freedom in that area you listed. Once you have finished, cut the paper down the line and throw the left side away. Keep the right side up as a reminder that you are a new creation, living in the spirit and mystery of the great love of our lives.

After you have completed the action, take three deep breaths and repeat this phrase:

I accept the sacred orientation that is my knowing deep down. I acknowledge that I am loved and supported by the forces governing my universe, and I am a conduit of this love and support for myself and for others. I choose to love myself fully, to accept my past as part of my divine journey, and to forgive, appreciate, and embrace all the people, places, and things in my life as my access to that divine love. I orient myself now to my truth, my power, and my love within, and I author my life in a co-creative way that serves my highest good as well as the highest good of all those around me, free from any and all fears or doubts. I am my most authentic self, and I express myself fully as such to create a life I love. And so, it is.

"BE WHO YOU ARE
AND SAY WHAT YOU FEEL,
BECAUSE THOSE WHO MIND
DON'T MATTER, AND THOSE
WHO MATTER DON'T MIND."

— *Dr. Seuss*

CHAPTER 6

SLEEPING WITH A MARRIED WOMAN

From the time I was told that God was a big invisible judge in the sky, I was determined to validate this as the truth.

The way I "proved" my own truth was to make my actions subject to someone else's scrutiny, which enabled me to play the role of the victim in the story.

Yet deep within my victim mentality lurked my desire to be the martyr as well.

Because of the attention I got.

When that invisible judge in the sky was unavailable (which was always), I would create a situation where I could say, "Look what blah blah blah did to me."

"Woe is me!"

"Feel sorry for me!"

"I am SUCH a survivor; aren't I so strong and brave?"

"Isn't blah blah blah worse than me?"

It didn't matter what the offense or who the offender was, I stopped at nothing to be right...to make someone ELSE wrong...and to make sure that all those around me were aware that I was the one suffering in the process.

"Taking up my cross for Jesus" I made sure everyone knew I was earning holiness points.

Except that this time around, sleeping with a married woman meant that I got to be the sinner.

I got to be on the other side.

For once in my life, I got to have the power.

Or so I thought.

The situation for me to sleep with a married woman presented itself relatively easily.

She was in an open marriage at the time, so sleeping with her didn't feel like that big of an offense.

Her marriage "didn't count" in my book, and I was separated, so in my mind I told myself that I was "pretty much divorced."

I told myself I deserved it.

I deserved to NOT be the victim for once.

"I am vanquished from all my offenders," I told myself.

But underneath that thought, do you know who/what was running the show?

The victim.

Oh, the irony.

I am reminded of the saying, "You can put lipstick on a pig, and it's still a pig."

The reality was that I was so desperate to make up for the story I was telling myself that something was wrong with me, that I would take anyone who would have me, male or female...gay or straight...married or single.

Why?

Well, not only are victims desperate for attention, they are desperate for victory.

And any conquest would have done for me...and continued to do for me...for many years.

The truth is though, regardless of who I was sleeping with, and no matter what side of the fence I was on, I was betraying MYSELF.

It didn't matter -- betrayal was my experience in one way, shape, or form.

I was betraying what I really wanted...and who I really was.

In the game of life, inauthenticity was my sport.

I had lots of teams and lots of players.

To these players I was saying, "I can't trust you."

When in reality I was saying, "I can't trust me."

For what we say to others, we're really saying to ourselves.

This truth hit me years later when I experienced another betrayal, and got to honestly face the common denominator in all my relationships:

ME.

((insert laughter and tears))

So, I decided right then and there that I was going to trust myself.

To believe in the real me.

That small voice.

That big presence.

The intuition to move.

Knowing when to run.

And knowing when to slow down.

Feeling when it's time to leap.

And feeling when it's time to stop.

As I began to trust myself, I began to detox the negative energy around sex and my sexuality.

Even though it had been years and they had since divorced, I felt I HAD to confess my behavior to the man who was the husband of the woman I slept with.

It was a night at least five years later and I found myself in a room where he was my ayahuasca shaman.

Spirit medicine has a hilarious way of clearing out guilt and shame.

After the ceremony, I could not shake the feeling that a confession was in order, so I told him.

And you know what?

It didn't matter to him.

And I understood in that moment...that it only mattered to ME.

I was the one making the whole sh*t show significant.

It was MY conversation around secrecy and hiding that gave the whole story its power.

And the beautiful part was, that in my willingness to show the sh*t, the drama of it all began to lessen.

The anxiety subsided.

I saw that opening the door on my shadow is what let more light into the room.

More light to trust.

More light to let go.

More light to leap.

And more light to love.

Love myself...love others...and love the truth.

Sky grandpa wasn't around, but I sure was proud.

GIFT 6:
EMBRACE LIES AS ACCESS TO TRUTHS

This one could take a while to unpack, as there are so many untruths out there, and so many secrets we're hiding. The key I want to leave you with regarding this is that no matter what the truth is that we believe, we will validate it. And, we have to experience untruths for us to understand/ appreciate the power of the truth.

For years I was subject to the scrutiny of an invisible force that judged me, and because of that, I became my OWN judge. And then I would create situations/stories for me to be the betrayed, the betrayer, or both. But I wouldn't have gotten to ANY of what I feel to be grander/bigger truths if I had not first lied to myself, been lied to, and lied to others.

Appreciating that lies are our access to truths is not a means to justify our insincerity or lack of authenticity either. It's merely a means for us to stop feeling guilty over the past. To move past being the victim AND the martyr. Embracing it all as a gift enables our freedom from toxic behavior toward ourselves as well as toward others.

APPLICATION

Ask yourself, are there areas in your life where you are holding on to a belief that feels untrue? If so, what are those untruths?

____

____

How would your life go if you held on to this way of being and continued your current course of actions?

What do you see happening if you chose to rewrite a new story?

INSPIRED ACTION:

CONFESS! I know, six chapters in and I'm asking you to put yourself out there already. But if you want to do the work of personal freedom, you've got to be willing to free yourself.

Only you know what could be weighing on you. This could be making amends, but it also could just be getting clear with someone on something minor that you have not been authentic about.

We lie all the time with our excuses. Were we really too busy to send an email reply yesterday and that was the reason we didn't? Then why do we say it? Because saying, "I didn't get around to it" or, "I didn't make it a priority" makes us look bad.

Being honest means we get to risk looking bad.

So, if there's something there for you that occurs to you like, "I don't want to do that, it'll make me look bad," do it today. Consider this your sign from the universe!

After you have completed the action, take three deep breaths and repeat this phrase:

I accept the sacred orientation that is my knowing deep down. I acknowledge that I am loved and supported by the forces governing my universe, and I am a conduit of this love and support for myself and for others. I choose to love myself fully, to accept my past as part of my divine journey, and to forgive, appreciate, and embrace all the people, places, and things in my life as my access to that divine love. I orient myself now to my truth, my power, and my love within, and I author my life in a co-creative way that serves my highest good as well as the highest good of all those around me, free from any and all fears or doubts. I am my most authentic self, and I express myself fully as such to create a life I love. And so, it is.

"THERE IS NOTHING NOBLE
IN BEING SUPERIOR
TO YOUR FELLOW MEN.
TRUE NOBILITY LIES
IN BEING SUPERIOR
TO YOUR FORMER SELF."

— Ernest Hemingway

CHAPTER 7

WARM HUGS, HOT COFFEE

"What's with you?" my ex-wife asked me as I voluntarily (as well as genuinely) hugged her and said, "I just love you!"

It had only been seven or so months since I was throwing all her things out of her dresser, attempting to kick her out of the house, threatening evictions and issuing restraining orders.

And there I was within the same year, at her apartment just a few buildings from mine, swapping out the children and showing her genuine affection.

Key word, GENUINE.

Which is what caught her off guard and created her confusion.

"What IS with me?!" I thought — yeah, makes sense she'd feel like she was in the presence of someone she never knew.

For years my feelings had been forced — an obligatory expression.

Also stated, I was full of sh*t.

"Do the right thing and love" I'd normally tell myself and push through day by day, staying in a marriage that wasn't working.

But this time, the feelings weren't forced at all.

On this day, the world was in color.

And no one and no thing was going to tell me anything to the contrary.

For the first time in my life, at the age of 35, I had fallen in love.

Rainbows were literally everywhere.

I met him at a networking event and I had my typical, "Who is THAT?!" response, so I made sure to set a "Get to know each other's business" coffee meeting, which conveniently I only had to wait three days for.

And that "meeting" quickly turned into an almost four-hour dive into each other's souls, going way deeper than any business conversation I'd ever had, and certainly more intimate than any other date I'd had up until that point as well.

"I want to see you again" I declared with glee toward the end of our time together.

"Me too" he quipped with matched enthusiasm.

I called him maybe two minutes after we parted ways.

“Do you miss me?” I asked, not really caring what he said, and excited to hear his answer.

“I do!” he answered with excitement.

What followed was a whirlwind of connection, chemistry, and adventure.

Up until this point, I had never had the experience of mutual attraction.

Normally tormented by thinking, “This is wrong and not allowed,” I had always had “secret” crushes, yet never acted on them.

Affection that was equally shared was a faraway dream, separated by my guilt and lack of permission.

So, finding him was nothing less than magical.

It didn’t matter that I didn’t know him that well.

Nearly middle-aged, and it was like I’d never been kissed.

And I was in love.

The past with the ex-wife?

IRRELEVANT!

The fights...screams...holes in walls...drunken sobs of sadness...affairs and near death experiences of dramatic depression?

WHO CARES!!!

I was literally buzzing wherever I went.

Shortly after I gave my ex that unrequested and equally sincere hug and declaration of love, I ended up telling her about my experience with him, which is something I NEVER could have imagined me doing.

“Good!” she said, “I’m happy for you.”

And ironically, I believed her.

I got it.

She had found someone as well, so everything was making sense to me now.

“Oh, THIS is what it’s all about!” I’d think to myself.

“THIS is what was missing with her and me! DUH! No wonder we were miserable!”

I fascinated myself with my own revelation and glee.

So, what happened after that you may be asking yourself?

Ridiculously long story short, he began to distance himself, and eventually ignored me.

Literally ghosted, I was left to my own devices on how I was going to move on.

Our first coffee break lead to my first broken heart.

And, it’s a heart that is healed.

He could have ignored me because he was HIV positive and I was not, or it could have been for some other reason.

He cut me out before I could cut him out (or so he presumed would occur).

See friend, the relationship journey always involves someone else's sacred path as well, so who knows how long we'll be sharing our time together.

To have joy in a relationship, it can only ever be about enjoying the time that is shared, for however long you experience it, because nothing lasts forever.

That time of love was amazing for me, and it was so I could get it, show that love, share that love, and move on.

That is the beauty of love.

It heals us without even trying.

Apart from our effort or logic, love just IS.

Even seven years later, I still love that experience.

This is how I know that my heart is healed.

And I am thankful.

Even though it wasn't the "happily ever after" ending you might expect, it was and IS, the happiness I was looking for.

I often find myself contemplating these chapters in this book...in my life.

I can get sidetracked by trying to make a grandiose point, attempting to "find the point" about how to reconcile a story and create a "worthwhile finale" for you.

Thus, missing the point...that there is no point.

Reconciling my stories isn't about reconciling a relationship with a man.

It's not about a woman either.

It's about me.

It's about you.

And it's about us all.

Reconciling ourselves not only to our Creator(s).

But to Ourselves.

And to all of it.

The end is, that there is no end.

There is no beginning either.

We get to be done with the pursuit of having to have it all figured out, and just get to dancing.

Dancing in the rain, the sun, the mud, and the flowers.

We get to fall in love with this beautiful sh*t show called life.

Because Life — is only Love.

And it is meant to be hugged like there's no tomorrow.

So, "what's with me" you may ask?

The same that's with us all: Everything.

GIFT 7:
EMBRACE DISCONNECTION AS ACCESS TO CONNECTION

"Falling in love" can take many forms. I personally feel we are here as a species not just to find the love of our lives, but to BE the love of our lives. And, to love ALL of how life shows up. I stumbled upon this lover by "accident," and the deeper lesson I got out of the experience was not, "Love will show up when you least expect it," rather that our existence is meant to be that joyful, that blissful, that enjoyable.

For me, I received that experience because I was in a space of full self-acceptance and self-expression before I met him. Might I meet someone like him again? More than likely yes, and as you'll see later, I actually did! But there is no way I would have had the degree of rapture that I did had I not first made the step to be fully myself and connect to who I am.

So, this exercise is about embracing the times we felt disconnected, as a means to receive our connection to ourselves and to others. We could have felt disconnected from a previous or current lover, a parent/authority figure, or anyone else we deep down wanted to feel connected to.

Keep in mind that all feelings of disconnection are triggers for us to connect to OURSELVES first, so that is what embracing this gift is all about.

Connecting, finding, and embracing yourself.

APPLICATION

Ask yourself, are there areas in your life where you are holding on to a belief that says you are still disconnected from yourself or others? If so, what or who are they?

How would your life go if you held on to this way of being and continued your current course of actions?

What do you see happening if you chose to rewrite a new story?

____

____

____

____

____

INSPIRED ACTION:

We're gonna get dirty! Sort of. Today is your chance to get into the ground. I want you to do todays' affirmation outside with your bare feet on the ground. If it's muddy, even better. If it's cold outside, still do it; you'll feel alive. The longer you can do it, the better. Try to meditate/keep your eyes closed and take deep breaths. Feel your connection to the earth. Feel that you came from it, and you'll go back to it. You are like a tree in motion. Some trees are skinny. Some are fat. Some are tall, some are short. They can all be different shapes, colors, and be in different cycles of their development. They are perfect just as they are, the same way you are perfect just as you are. Breathe that in and feel your connection to all that is. You are a process. This is a process. You are growing, changing, and transforming always. Connect to ALL of it, and ALL of your experience. Bonus points if you hug and/or tell a tree that you love it!

After you have completed the action, take three deep breaths and repeat this phrase:

I accept the sacred orientation that is my knowing deep down. I acknowledge that I am loved and supported by the forces governing my universe, and I am a conduit of this love and support for myself and for others. I choose to love myself fully, to accept my past as part of my divine journey, and to forgive, appreciate, and embrace all the people, places, and things in my life as my access to that divine love. I orient myself now to my truth, my power, and my love within, and I author my life in a co-creative way that serves my highest good as well as the highest good of all those around me, free from any and all fears or doubts. I am my most authentic self, and I express myself fully as such to create a life I love. And so, it is.

"POOR IS THE MAN WHOSE PLEASURES DEPEND ON THE PERMISSION OF ANOTHER."

— *Madonna*

CHAPTER 8

PEACE TREES & DRUNK DRIVERS

Strolling along the French Quarter's Jackson Square, a piece of art stopped me dead in my tracks.

It was oil on canvas, at least four feet wide by five feet tall.

An amazing oak tree with leaves filling and creating the shape of a heart, adorned in the most vivid and translucent hues of browns, oranges and reds.

As I looked at it, its beauty spoke to a part of me that I didn't know I had.

If you've never been to Jackson Square in New Orleans, it's an eclectic mix of street vendors, musicians, and artists.

On this day, the sound of jazz filled the air as tourists and locals buzzed about their business.

The only thing that made today any different was that it was my birthday.

Which, according to creole tradition, meant that the locals pinned dollar bills to my shirt.

I had been flooded with money and love from strangers already, and that was before my breath was taken away by that oak heart.

After a moment to compose myself, I struck up a conversation with the artist who was standing next to it.

A gypsy woman (a lot of them in the Quarter are), complete with the flowy skirt, crimped hair, and weathered skin that showed signs of equal indulgences in sun, booze, and cigarettes.

However, her soul...her eyes, were exquisite.

She had found her peace.

And I was captivated.

Throughout our conversation, this one statement of hers made the hair on the back of my neck stand up.

Goose pimples wouldn't be sufficient.

God-pimples I'll call them.

"You know something baby?" she asked with whimsy and glee. "I may not have everything I want, but I have everything I need."

The words activated something in my core.

Through her bright smile yet lackluster teeth, she delivered that statement with such contentment and joy.

Right there in front of me, selling her stuff on the street.

She saw me.

Or rather, I felt seen.

And it was in this moment I knew I had to quit my job.

I had just gotten divorced and had the pleasure of also adding foreclosure and bankruptcy to my life resume.

It was not a time in my life where resources were abundant. In fact, it was one of my best friends who all but practically paid for my gas to get me to the city for my birthday.

There was no safety net.

Hell, there was barely a fishing line.

During my job hunt, being a former business owner actually hurt me, as I heard, "You're just too overqualified" on almost a daily basis.

This pretty much meant that the only job I managed to secure was telemarketing, which paid next to nothing.

It was not the best job. It was not the worst job.

However, the company had revamped their calling script, and had taken on limited integrity in their selling methods.

I knew deep down that I was out of alignment.

Ah yes, the knowing deep down.

I had only been working about six weeks when I encountered that wise gypsy with the knack for colors and for speaking into my soul, confirming that my time at this employer was going to be short.

What father quits his job with no knowledge of where the next paycheck is going to come from?

Apparently, me.

When Monday rolled around and I got back home from my enlightened vacation, my boss declared in a meeting that we all needed to commit to better numbers -- to write down on the white board what we were committed to.

I sunk in my chair.

It was do or die.

Or in this case, leave or lie.

I could not in good faith commit to something that I knew was not helping the people I was selling to.

Translated, I sneaked out the conference room back door.

However, on my way out I ran into one of my bosses.

Never in my career had I quit on the spot, face-to-face like that.

My blood was literally racing through my body, and I knew it was the right thing to do.

And before I knew it, I was in my car.

"What are you going to do for money?" I thought to myself as I left the building for the last time.

Self-deprecating thoughts began to race through my head.

"Your vehicle has expired inspection, needs new tires, new brakes, and has a crack in the windshield. What the f*ck are you doing with your life?

Why did you do that? You're such an idiot!"

And before I knew it, SLAM!

She came out of nowhere.

The airbag deployed as I simultaneously slammed on the brakes, and in an instant I was stopped in the middle of a three-lane road.

Turns out she had been drinking, so she was taken to the hospital.

Although my car was totaled, I walked away unscathed.

And by the end of the week insurance pulled through, I had a new car, and a few months' worth of income on top of it.

Just enough to get me and my business off the ground.

It wasn't everything I wanted.

And it was everything I needed.

Whether or not I see that painting ever again is irrelevant compared to the most beautiful thing I received out of that whole experience.

My faith created my peace.

God really did have my back.

What art my life has been ever since.

What art your life can be.

And what art we can paint together.

GIFT 8:
EMBRACE FEAR AS ACCESS TO FAITH

Honestly, this could be a whole book in and of itself. Now that I think about it, all these gifts of contrast could be book topics! A common theme of limited self-expression is fear. And in this case, the part of me that wanted to be expressed was the entrepreneur, and the version of me that was in the way was the employee. I have hinted on this before, that I am not advocating that anyone with the itch to start their own business should quit their job; I am advocating for you to follow WHEREVER your heart leads you.

For me, I knew beforehand that job wasn't for me. The more I worked there, the more time I wasted. The trip to New Orleans just sealed the deal, and then at the meeting the following Monday there was just no way I could have stayed if I was also going to be committed to myself.

We always have a choice though. In reality, I could have stayed at that job. I could have lied and come up with some bogus sales targets. I could have also stayed in my marriage or stayed living where I did, but I did not. I signed up for an adventure, and I have a bit of good news/bad news here love, because you're reading this, you signed up for it too.

And all great adventure involves faith. And not just small faith. Big faith. I'm not speaking of religious faith here; I am speaking in the power of belief. In the knowing that regardless of evidence of outside circumstance, what you choose to believe in is BIGGER and is the actual truth. And stepping into this truth always, and I mean always, requires dancing with fear.

But since you've already done something that scares you, and confessed something to someone, this chapter's assignment is about the fun part of faith: Vision. Because when we know where we're headed, we're more likely to get there, and more likely to dance with and overcome that fear along the way.

APPLICATION

Ask yourself, are there areas in your life where you are holding on to a belief that says you can or cannot do something? If so, what are they?

How would your life go if you held on to this way of being and continued your current course of actions?

____

____

____

____

What do you see happening if you chose to rewrite a new story?

____

____

____

____

INSPIRED ACTION:

If you have never done a vision board, this is your time! If you have, this is a chance to revisit it, edit it, or add to it. The beauty of vision boarding is that it is the first step to calling into matter that which does not yet exist. Based on my mentor Wayne Dyer's advice, I did it for this book. I printed off a cover graphic and pasted it onto some other book. I made it real before it was "real." I've done it for years and have executed a number of things -- vacations, TEDx talks, you name it! Not all have come true, yet, but that's part of the process.

So, take some time and clip some magazines if you have them. Make an image using google photos if you have access to a computer as most of us do. Make it fun. The key is to FEEL the feeling of that which you desire. To acknowledge what you are desiring, and to not stay in the feeling of wanting. I heard it called the law of satisfaction once, as opposed to the law of attraction you hear so much about.

Picture it -- make an actual picture of it -- and then take time to feel how it would feel to be the person who has those things. The magic is in the embodiment of future you. And the last technique to it is to picture who you are AFTER all those things are added to your life. Who would you be? What would you think? How would you FEEL if you really were done-done? Look at your pictures, then embody THAT person.

After you have completed the action, take three deep breaths and repeat this phrase:

I accept the sacred orientation that is my knowing deep down. I acknowledge that I am loved and supported by the forces governing my universe, and I am a conduit of this love and support for myself and for others. I choose to love myself fully, to accept my past as part of my divine journey, and to forgive, appreciate, and embrace all the people, places, and things in my life as my access to that divine love. I orient myself now to my truth, my power, and my love within, and I author my life in a co-creative way that serves my highest good as well as the highest good of all those around me, free from any and all fears or doubts. I am my most authentic self, and I express myself fully as such to create a life I love. And so, it is.

"THE CREDIT BELONGS TO THE MAN WHO IS ACTUALLY IN THE ARENA...WHO AT THE WORST, IF HE FAILS, AT LEAST FAILS WHILE DARING GREATLY, SO THAT HIS PLACE SHALL NEVER BE WITH THOSE COLD AND TIMID SOULS WHO NEITHER KNOW VICTORY NOR DEFEAT."

— *Theodore Roosevelt*

CHAPTER 9

CLOSETS AREN'T MADE FOR THE WEAK

"Ok God, I just need this one deal to close, and I'll be good," I thought to myself as I attempted to reconcile my bills on a Monday night.

I was about $6,000 short on my expenses that month and had a real estate deal that was scheduled to close within days, so I was biding my time (and avoiding phone calls) until the settlement occurred.

Come the next day though, the deal fell apart.

As in, zero dollars.

I had already sold my living room furniture, dining room furniture, and was sleeping on an air mattress.

I had half a loaf of bread and some spaghetti in the pantry.

Ironically and/or congruently, I had been led to give away 10% of whatever I made, and it occurred to me that I was $10 short on what I was supposed to have given to my faith community that previous Sunday.

I went to check my account before I submitted the $10 payment.

Twenty dollars in my account.

Twenty.Effin.Dollars.

My mind raced. “Really ‘God?’ You gonna go like that? I gotta give HALF of what I have left, and it only leaves me with 10 freaking dollars?”

“Well, I’m not the one who made the commitment,” the outside/inside voice answered.

I swear, God is such a smart ass.

(Sidebar, this is why I love him/her/it/me)

“Ok, fine, have it your way,” I protested as I clicked to pay my way to delusion.

Not exactly sure what I was going to do next, I just kind of sat there staring at the screen for who knows how long.

Freshly divorced, I had divided up all our “stuff,” and sold or given away most everything else as part of the downsizing process.

And looking at my practically empty apartment, I seriously wondered what was left to sell.

“Oh my gosh! I have a carpet cleaner, that’ll give me $40 I bet. That’s a tank of gas and beans and rice!”

It’s amazing how little it takes to excite me.

As I went to pull out the carpet cleaner from the kids closet, I found a box under a box.

Something I had completely forgotten about.

It was a collection of silver coins.

They were the Smithsonian presidential commemorative ones too.

My father had given them to me when I got married, and I kind of just carried them from house to house, or in this most recent case, house to apartment.

"Oh my gosh," I said to myself, "I can't believe I forgot about these! If they're worth a couple of hundred dollars, I am going to lose my sh*t!"

I quickly inspected the collection and scurried my way to my computer to check eBay to investigate whether or not there was something comparable on the market.

As I typed the description, a listing for sale came up with a buy-it-now price.

You're not going to believe it.

$6,000.

That's right, I said it.

$6,000.

After practically soiling myself, I double checked all the weights of the coins and the silver trading weight to confirm, and there I had it in black and white.

Provision.

Manna.

Buried deep in my closet.

Turns out, the kingdom of heaven sort of IS within.

The irony was just too incredibly laughable.

Smart ass gods are too deliciously hilarious for words sometimes.

The next day I cashed in those coins and paid my bills like a champ.

It was a lesson in remembering who I was and who I was playing this game with:

A freaking amazing coach.

See friend, none of us make it out of this sh*t show alive.

We all die.

So, the question begs, do you want to die on the bench or die on the field?

The field is where your blood and guts are, but guess what, that's where Life is found too.

On the field of giving.

Giving when it's not comfortable.

Giving when it costs you something.

Giving because you know deep down that we're not in this alone, and in that experience, feeling so freaking alive.

Giving is not our motivation to receive, but our access to receive.

We dance and play together, for it's all the same energy.

So let's play ball, shall we?

GIFT 9: EMBRACE GIVING AS ACCESS TO RECEIVING

Giving and receiving are the same energy; it is an exchange. You cannot possibly do one without the other. It's a constant flow that must maintain equilibrium. It's an offering, and we indeed reap what we sow. Any time you want more of anything, you must give something in order to make way to receive. The challenge I have seen in my life is twofold. One was my motivation to give. If I give X dollars with the desire/hope/wish that I am to receive that or more back, what I was *really* offering was an attitude of "give me." The stronger/more dominant vibration/intention was the expectation to receive. So, what I received was just more desire to receive! Oh, the irony.

The second challenge was that what I wanted to receive I felt I had to give the same thing -- meaning, if I wanted money, I gave money. But that is not the case when it comes to energy. I can give ANY NUMBER of things -- my time, my voice, my service, etc. For MOST of us, giving money is the most powerful thing we can do because it's the thing we have the most attachment too, but it is the OFFERING that counts.

The keys I realized were to give with zero expectations of WHAT I was to receive, HOW I was to receive, or WHEN I was to receive. To give for the sake of giving, to be willing to be used, and to be willing to receive -- dancing with faith, trust, surrender, and joy.

APPLICATION

Ask yourself, what areas in your life or things are you holding on to or not giving away?

____

____

____

____

____

How would your life go if you held on to this way of being and continued your current course of actions?

____

____

____

____

____

What do you see happening if you chose to rewrite a new story?

____

____

____

____

INSPIRED ACTION:

Well you guessed it -- you gotta give! For most people, the most powerful thing we can give is money, however the key is that no matter what it is, it must cost you something. The only time we grow is when we push ourselves out of our comfort zones. The task today is to give something that feels like a sacrifice to do so. And remember, you don't give in order to receive. You give for offering's sake, and make it a testament to your faith, trust, and surrender to the process of all of it.

After you have completed the action, take three deep breaths and repeat this phrase:

I accept the sacred orientation that is my knowing deep down. I acknowledge that I am loved and supported by the forces governing my universe, and I am a conduit of this love and support for myself and for others. I choose to love myself fully, to accept my past as part of my divine journey, and to forgive, appreciate, and embrace all the people, places, and things in my life as my access to that divine love. I orient myself now to my truth, my power, and my love within, and I author my life in a co-creative way

that serves my highest good as well as the highest good of all those around me, free from any and all fears or doubts. I am my most authentic self, and I express myself fully as such to create a life I love. And so, it is.

"PERSEVERANCE
IS A GREAT
ELEMENT OF SUCCESS.
IF YOU KNOCK
LONG ENOUGH
AND LOUD ENOUGH
AT THE GATE,
YOU ARE SURE TO WAKE
SOMEBODY UP."

— *Henry Wadsworth Longfellow*

CHAPTER 10

FOOD TRUCKS & FAITH BOMBS

It was two days before the first event I ever produced that I encountered the business breakdown of a lifetime.

Over 60 food trucks were all competing for $10,000, and not only was I producing the entire 6-day event, I was personally sponsoring the grand prize with money from other real estate deals/income I had in the pipeline.

Then at the last minute, one of those deals fell through.

With less than 48 hours to go, I was $8,000 short.

At this point I had some "easy" choices -- fetal position -- quit -- vodka/Benadryl -- prostitution -- throw myself off a cliff...

Or the best/easiest one for the youngest child to do...

Run to mommy.

Not for money, but for a conversation.

She's always been my rock for those times.

Regardless of our differences regarding Christianity and sexual orientation, we always managed to find a way not to burn bridges, but to build them.

Which included this pivotal conversation.

"Do you know this is what God wants you to be doing?" she asked with staunch conviction (so funny how moms ask questions they already know the answers to).

I had been working on it for over 9 months, and had come SO FAR, that there was NO WAY that I could say anything other than, "Yes!"

"Well, there you go, there's your mustard seed," she said without missing a beat.

She followed it up with the point, "If faith required a blueprint, it would not be faith at all."

It was one of those, "thanks a lot mom/eye roll/know your parent is right" moments.

However, it was enough to pull myself out of the fetal position, and I PRESSED ON.

I decided that I was NOT going down without knowing that I did EVERYTHING in my power to promote the hell (literally) out of this event.

I sent out what may have been my 6th press release at 2AM, and I continued to harass all my friends and family to spread the word.

And the DAY BEFORE the event, do you know what happened?

We ended up getting picked up on all 4 TV stations.

We went from less than 100 tickets to over 1500 tickets... from $2,000 to $30,000 in about 24 hours.

It was beautiful and chaotic and beautiful.

My problem shifted from, "How am I even going to do this," to, "How am I going to manage all these people?"

And manage it we did.

If this experience taught me anything, it was that anything is possible -- ALWAYS.

See, not everything about my religious past was bad.

Some things were brilliant.

"If you have faith as small as a mustard seed, you can say to this mountain, 'Move from here to there,' and it will move. Nothing will be impossible for you."

"Ask, and it is given."

"Seek, and ye shall find."

"Knock, and the door will be opened unto you."

These were but a few universal truths of God revealed to me that first year being in business.

I'll always remember that conversation that was larger than life, and smaller than a mustard seed.

For I asked, and it was given.

I sought, and it was found.

And I definitely knocked on that door, and it was flung wide open.

I am beyond grateful not just for that day, but for every day thereafter.

They are all a gift, and I kinda don't like blueprints anyway.

GIFT 10:
EMBRACE QUITTING AS ACCESS TO SUCCESS

Here's the deal. Everything boils down to imagination. We are making all of this up. Most of us default to imagining/picturing the worst possible outcome, and that's not how it has to be. Most people convince themselves at some point that it's too hard and the price of continuing feels harder than stopping. But we only stop because we're believing the doom and gloom picture of the future that we created.

What I did not include in this story was that I had spent months of listening to an audio recording I had made of myself in the future, as the festival in the past. It was a future that was pulling for me.

When I had that conversation with my mother, I did not think about my audio and that my future must come to pass. I literally could only think how impossible it felt. But when she told me I just needed to have that mustard seed of faith, that was enough for me to get back into action.

Because deep down, I knew what quitting would get me. Imagining the quitting outcome is easy for so many, particularly those who have any commitment to martyrdom or suffering like I did because of my dogmatic understanding of God. And knowing even deeper down that the quitting story was not something I wanted, I manifested my mother as my support in that moment.

You know what success is only because you know what quitting will get you, so choose and imagine a picture that works for you, and ACT AS IF it already is, for you will indeed receive that which you prepare for. An amazing book for resetting your money game, particularly if you are looking to overcome negative religious narratives is, "The Game of Life and How to Play It" by Florence Scovel Shinn.

APPLICATION

Ask yourself, are there areas in your life where you are holding on to a belief that says quitting is inevitable, or the default solution? If you've quit in the past, what results did you get?

____

____

____

____

____

____

How would your life go if you held on to this way of being and continued your current course of actions?

____

____

____

____

What do you see happening if you chose to rewrite a new story?

____

____

____

____

INSPIRED ACTION:

So, you have a vision of where you want to go, and you also need to be prepared to go all sorts of ways you didn't expect to get there. There is beauty in mystery in allowing yourself to be surprised. I am reminded of Matthew 7:7, "Ask and it will be given to you; seek and you will find; knock and the door will be opened to you." Here we see the only action we're required to do is knock. Which is priceless advice for obtaining success no matter what you're doing. You have to knock on those doors. There is no morality in it, it's all a simple numbers game.

For this task, breathe into what you want to ask for, and what doors you want to knock on. If you already know, get to knocking. If you've already been knocking, knock some more. Today is not the day to quit. If you normally knock on one door, knock on two. If you normally knock on ten, knock on twenty. Today is the day to do one more thing, not the day to give up. To go to bed knowing that you did absolutely everything in your power to reach your goal. You persist, and you succeed.

After you have completed the action, take three deep breaths and repeat this phrase:

I accept the sacred orientation that is my knowing deep down. I acknowledge that I am loved and supported by the forces governing my universe, and I am a conduit of this love and support for myself and for others. I choose to love myself fully, to accept my past as part of my divine journey, and to forgive, appreciate, and embrace all the people, places, and things in my life as my access to that divine love. I orient myself now to my truth, my power, and my love within, and I author my life in a co-creative way that serves my highest good as well as the highest good of all those around me, free from any and all fears or doubts. I am my most authentic self, and I express myself fully as such to create a life I love. And so, it is.

"PEOPLE DO NOT
SEEM TO REALIZE
THAT THEIR OPINION
OF THE WORLD
IS ALSO A CONFESSION
OF CHARACTER."

— Ralph Waldo Emerson

CHAPTER 11

SOUL MATES AT CHIPOTLE

The day was full of color and promise.

The bills were paid.

There was money in the bank.

The weather was amazing...cool and warm, brisk as well as sunny.

Life was...full of color.

Beyond unstoppable.

Blissfully beautiful.

Coming back from yoga, there was literally nothing that could hinder my happiness as I waltzed my way into Chipotle.

So blissed out that I didn't even look at my phone while I stood in line, I beamed while I gave my order to the workers behind the line and smiled in gratitude to the cashier as I paid my bill.

And then I saw him.

One of the better-looking men I've seen in my day.

"Wow, it IS a beautiful day," I thought to myself.

And then he looked at me.

We actually met eyes.

"Did he just look at me?" I began to frantically assess in my mind.

I feverishly continue my inner monologue, "Even though he's sitting with another guy and a girl, I'm going to walk by him again just to make sure he checked me out."

"Yep, he definitely looked at me because he's looking at me right now" I thought as I practically skipped passed him.

As I scurried to my table to attempt to eat without mental obsession, it inevitably happened.

The mental gerbil wheel of conversation determined to get me to go up to him and give him my card.

Except I didn't have any cards on me.

I got stopped for a minute but then realized that I do NOT make excuses!

I went out to my car to write my name and number on a sheet of paper to give to him.

My mind raced along with its own conversations and shutdowns. "This isn't desperate at all, right? Don't answer that."

As I finished writing my information down, he ended up walking out with his guests toward their cars.

I said to myself, "Okay, going up to him at this point is straight up creepy at this point. I'd have to chase him down in the parking lot. The time has passed. Let it go. It's not like he's the last attractive person on the planet."

And so, I let it go, determined that I was going to carry my cards with me wherever I went, as to have plenty of time to pounce on the next unsuspecting prey.

Apparently, this was my dating strategy: I was willing to put myself out there, old-school style.

Vintage risk.

I could dig it.

Learning...growing...moving.

A couple of weeks later I was out to eat with my kids, and I started laughing to myself at this crazy idea of mine.

"What are you laughing at dad?" my then 8-year-old son asked me.

I confessed, "Well, I came up with this game for me to meet new people. It's sort of like a game of tag, but for grownups."

"Hmm," he processed, "So, do you see anyone here you want to tag?"

At this point I am thinking I have an 8-year-old wingman... shame is only semi-present for me.

There was no one there taggable at the time, so I told him no.

And after another week or so, I still had not made a tag connection.

I was beginning to question this whole revolutionary strategy I had come up with.

But then I got a random Facebook message from a guy, and I thought to myself, "Wait, maybe I am the one who wants to be tagged!"

After a little bit of light Facebook stalking, I concluded that I was willing to accept his tag, and this was WAY better than sacrificing myself in public.

Screw vintage, I was going high tech.

My reply to him included an invite to coffee, to which he agreed almost immediately.

I was excited.

It was about 4 hours later in the middle of the night that it hit me though.

He was the guy from Chipotle.

That's right, I said it.

I was sure of it, however it was near 3 A.M. so I did not call or message him to confirm.

Which meant I just squealed my way through the apartment like a giddy schoolgirl three hours before dawn.

I slept maybe a few hours before messaging him and confirming that it was him.

He knew it was him because I told him what he was wearing, and who he was sitting with.

“Yep, that was me,” he said. “That was my favorite shirt that I thought I lost but actually found it that morning.”

This of course sent me into a completely dizzy adolescent melt down.

“I’ve found the one...I’m sure of it!” I giggled to myself.

And the three weeks that followed that revelation were a whirlwind.

We were both traveling outside of Austin, so we pretty much dated long distance.

I was visiting family in Virginia; he was in Colorado.

It was the first time I had been back to my former town since moving to Austin, coming out of the closet, and leaving my marriage.

My mindset was completely different than when I had lived there.

Who I was, a polar opposite of who I had been.

I was hypnotized by the magic of life.

Practically in love with possibility.

And do you know what I felt and “saw” when I was back there?

A parallel dimension.

I witnessed what would have been...what could have been had I not chosen authenticity.

I stood outside the house that I spent almost five years in, opened three restaurants and had two children in, and I saw my alternate life.

There was a family in my former house, MY house, making dinner...making a life.

And it *could have been* my life.

Part of me wonders if there's an alternate me still living there.

Yet it wasn't.

And I'm not.

Because I made the choice that I did.

To start over.

Which led me to start an authentic life.

There had been pain, for sure, and now the world was full of color and possibility.

Full color...and it was perfect, because the world...my world...was limitless.

But back to my Chipotle miracle man.

Do you know how that magical almost-relationship ended?

(and yes, it ended)

It ended because of shame.

His shame as well as mine, as we are all reflections of each other.

We were out to eat, and he didn't want to be seen too close to me because he saw someone from his church there.

It was subtle, and I felt limited.

Hidden.

And if I know one thing, I know that I did not come out of the closet to hide.

Any time, any place, I will be fully me.

So as magical as that relationship started, it was time for it to end.

I learned that there was no problem with him, but that it was me who got to be bolder about my sexual orientation and the truth about who I am.

And I was reminded that everything is a reflection.

Everything.

And it's all for our learning.

Whether a relationship is a day or a thousand days, we're here for each other's growth.

To grow OUT of shame, and INTO our true selves.

ALL of my experiences with my soul mate -- Chipotle, Facebook, connecting, appreciating, traveling...all of it, it was to bring CLOSURE to my old life, and to remind me of MAGIC.

Not just as a possibility, but as a reality.

And that we are ALL each other's soul mates.

THAT is the magic that I learned.

Every relationship, no matter how small, makes a ripple in the universe, and is our opportunity to connect with our own soul.

The date.

The cashier.

The bank teller.

The schoolteacher.

The telemarketer.

All of the mundane.

It's ALL magic.

And it's ALL love.

It is for us, and it IS us.

So, may we embrace ALL of it -- all of OURSELVES -- as the sweetest gift that it is and as the sweetest gift that we are.

GIFT 11: EMBRACE HOLDING ON AS ACCESS TO LETTING GO

The beauty of this whole story for me is toward the beginning when I wanted to give him my contact information but chose not to, and how just a few weeks later he found me. The magic that followed and what I got to learn from all of it was triggered by that letting go. There comes a time when we act, and there comes a time when we let go. I listened to that voice that said to let him go, and I truly was not attached to having to bring him back in the future. I believed that I'd meet whoever I would meet, whenever I would meet them. It was an agreement I made with the universe to play its game, and man was it fun. Even with the temporary pain of it not working out, what I gained from the process far outweighed any heartache. And, it left me more present to magic as a way of life, not just as an occasional occurrence.

Had I chased after him, had I forced a connection, or even if I had I held on to the idea of having to find him, the future would have gone COMPLETELY differently. I know the beauty, power, and magic of letting go because of the struggle and strife attached to the effort that's required to hold on.

Holding on takes so much energy, and when we let go of holding on, that energy is freed up to bring the cooperative components of the universe our way to support us with synchronicities in ways we could have never imagined.

APPLICATION

Ask yourself, are there areas in your life where you are holding on to anything or anyone? If so, what/who is it, and why?

____

____

____

____

____

How would your life go if you continued to hold on?

____

____

____

____

____

What do you see happening if you chose to rewrite a new story of letting go?

____

____

____

____

INSPIRED ACTION:

This is an exercise that may not feel like it's directly connected to the story, but the foundation of letting go is being secure in yourself, in knowing who you are, and being willing to play the surrender game with the forces that govern our universe. And as long as you're not secure in who you are, as long as you're not fully loving and accepting yourself just as you are, you will attempt to control the world and its circumstances as a means to compensate for your own lack of approval.

So, today's work is between you and you: The mirror.

If you've done mirror work before, it's always a good exercise, and if you have not done it before, it can transform your life.

When it comes to messages of love, we are usually the last ones to tell ourselves the things we enjoy telling other people, but today is the day to start telling yourself you are trustworthy, and worthy to be listened to.

Today you'll say the affirmation to the mirror. Say it as many times you need to, and end with an, "I love you."

Take three deep breaths and repeat this phrase while looking in the mirror:

I accept the sacred orientation that is my knowing deep down. I acknowledge that I am loved and supported by the forces governing my universe, and I am a conduit of this love and support for myself and for others. I choose to love myself fully, to accept my past as part of my divine journey, and to forgive, appreciate, and embrace all the people, places, and things in my life as my access to that

divine love. I orient myself now to my truth, my power, and my love within, and I author my life in a co-creative way that serves my highest good as well as the highest good of all those around me, free from any and all fears or doubts. I am my most authentic self, and I express myself fully as such to create a life I love. And so, it is.

And I love you.

"FORGIVE THEM,
FOR THEY KNOW NOT
WHAT THEY DO."

— *Luke 23:34*

CHAPTER 12

ABOMINABLE SNOWMEN & PUDDLES OF JOY

"You know it's an abomination, right?"

The words ripped through my soul as if an icicle had sliced me in half.

My breath was taken away by that frozen phrase from someone who claimed to be my family...by someone I considered my brother.

Not a week had gone by since I made the confession of my cruel demon....

The shadow that had chased me all my life....

My dark passenger....

My...flaw.

I had "same-sex attraction."

It was a phrase well-known in the religious/evangelical world in which I had grown up.

I wasn't gay...certainly not.

I was straight — with a problem.

For the most part, the fundamentalists believe that no one is born gay, and that anyone who expresses any desire for members of their same gender is a mutation of the nature of God's intention for humankind.

Therefore, my orientation became my "cross to bring to Jesus" to suffer through, and my relief would not be fully found until I died.

Hooray, where do I sign up?!

Before marriage I told my fiancé about my "old feelings," but said they were in the past, so I thought I was "over it."

Two years into our marriage I had a breakdown and confessed that I was "still dealing" with them, but neither of us had enough maturity or courage to actually deal with reality, so we swept it under the rug.

It wasn't until three years later that I reached this breaking point of truth:

No amount of sex with a woman was going to "cure my tendencies."

But now I had a thought — CONFESSION would.

It wasn't until this time in the marriage that I was willing to "come out," you might say.

But I wasn't declaring my freedom.

I was declaring my victimhood.

In the reparative therapy world, the way "out" of your same-sex attraction (remember, they do not believe in homosexual orientation), is to REPAIR where you went wrong by creating HEALTHY same-sex relationships.

So, I didn't need to leave my marriage.

I just needed to let everyone know I had issues.

And apparently have "conversations that matter" with the men in my life.

The basis for reparative/conversion therapy is that I was broken, and there was a plan to fix me.

The foundation of it is self-rejection (which is why it's now being outlawed in many states).

It is by far one of the unhealthiest things a human can go through.

So, as I sat there across the table from him, frozen stiff by that icicle dagger of a statement he delivered, the only thing that I could say in response to his opinion that homosexuality was an abomination was, "Yes, I know."

YES, I KNOW?

Did I just say, "Yes I know?"

My agreement sickened me.

Deep down I knew that wanting what we want is actually the furthest thing from an abomination, I just didn't have the courage to stand up and say it at the time.

So desperate to receive inclusion, so hungry to be loved and accepted, I agreed with the notion that my feelings were an affront to the Creator of them.

What followed that conversation were years of dysfunction.

In my relationship to my friends, family, wife, to almost everyone, and to myself.

Ego, ego, and more ego.

All the while betraying myself.

My true self.

The self that is perfect, whole, and complete, just the way it is.

The self that had a crush on his KINDERGARTEN classmate when I was SIX YEARS OLD.

The self that was playful, fun, and yes, into members of his same gender.

According to them, that self didn't matter.

That self was wrong.

Yes, that self was the abomination.

So clearly, I would create disasters, right?

What other option was there with that programming?

I ended up going into business with that family member, and then I subsequently ended up hiding money from him.

I was COMPLETELY out of integrity with myself.

Paying myself almost $30,000 more than I said I would and hoping none of the other partners would find out.

How in God's name was I going to create a business of alignment when I was out of alignment with myself?

Betrayal, betrayal, and more betrayal.

It didn't matter if it was family, a best friend, or a lover, I continued experiencing betrayal.

Because I was betraying MYSELF.

One chaotic mess after another led to the same dramatic conclusion:

I was fundamentally flawed.

So, I made sure to seal up my abominable fate and unintentionally allow that $30,000 secret to come to fruition.

My "accidental" email forward of a tax return to a family member revealed my inauthenticity and caused the proverbial sh*t to hit the fan.

I'll sum it up for you:

Chaos, chaos, and more chaos.

It was inevitable really.

Yet still, it was not beyond repair.

Fast forward ten years from that horrid conversation, through FINALLY coming out, divorcing my wife, and moving across the country, I found myself not only back where I was as a former member of the family, but standing in his living room like I still was, staring at artwork I had made years before, that he had mounted.

I had created it for his children, many years before our wretched confrontation.

And there it was hanging on the wall, staring at me through the eyes of children.

It was reconciliation at its finest.

A decade after being called an abomination I found myself in his home.

Sometimes words are not needed to heal, an invitation is.

An invitation to be welcomed.

An invitation to be included.

Life wasn't just about him including me no matter what.

It was about me including HIM no matter what.

He was enough.

I was enough.

He was a good man.

As was I.

And in that, we healed.

I understood in that moment that I am not here to burn bridges.

I am here to build them.

We all are.

We are not fundamentally flawed.

We are fundamentally fine.

Looking at the art and pictures I created, now hanging in his home, I felt honored to be there.

Honored to be accepted.

And honored to be me.

My heart was warm.

It's funny how icicles always seem to find their way to melt.

My abominable snowman...

Now my puddle of joy.

GIFT 12:
EMBRACE RESENTMENT AS ACCESS TO FORGIVENESS

When you can understand the power of forgiveness, you can heal not just yourself, but the world. One popular saying on the topic is, "Do you want to be right, or do you want to be free?" Or as Oprah has said on many occasions, "Not forgiving someone is like drinking poison and expecting someone else to die." The whole abomination comment probably didn't even bother the guy who said it, but I was letting it eat me alive...literally.

I had to process my forgiveness with myself first as well, before I could even think about forgiving him. But in that forgiving of him I forgave myself on an even deeper level.

And strange as it may sound, I got to a deeper level of self-love by embracing/not resisting the concept of resentment. I acknowledged that yes, I resented person X, Y, or Z for doing what they did, and from that space I could ask myself, "Now what?"

I let myself be angry, absolved myself from guilt, and gave myself (and the other permission) to move on.

Embracing it all is our gift.

Further reading on working through forgiveness can be found in, "Radical Forgiveness" by Colin Tipping. It's an amazing trip into how we create hurt in our lives as a means to experience the beauty of being free.

APPLICATION

Ask yourself, are you missing out on life because someone wronged you or told you that there was something wrong with you? This could be the way you look, your relationship status, or your career/work — wherever you feel like you've "fallen short" of your true potential? Or any kind of offense?

____

____

Write down a list of instances of who or where you adopted these ideas. Start with the most recent and move your way back. Take time to feel.

How would your life go if you held on to those stories and ran that program?

What do you see happening if you stopped and chose to rewrite a new program?

____

____

____

____

____

Write down new commitments and a new program that you are committed to running. Promise yourself to give yourself grace for the writing process.

____

____

____

____

INSPIRED ACTION:

Take at least ONE new step toward forgiveness and make an invitation if you can. If the person who has wronged you is still in your life, do whatever you need to do to forgive them. This does not mean having a have a conversation with them. Reconciliation is about getting complete with YOURSELF. You may need to involve them, you may not. The important thing to know is that forgiveness is about you, not them. You may need to forgive society, government, or God. It's about reconciling yourself to yourself, so make a choice right now to FINALLY let that someone off the hook. Tell them, "Thank you. I love you. Please forgive me, and I'm sorry."

After you have completed the action, take three deep breaths and repeat this phrase:

I accept the sacred orientation that is my knowing deep down. I acknowledge that I am loved and supported by the forces governing my universe, and I am a conduit of this love and support for myself and for others. I choose to love myself fully, to accept my past as part of my divine journey, and to forgive, appreciate, and embrace all the people, places, and things in my life as my access to that divine love. I orient myself now to my truth, my power, and my love within, and I author my life in a co-creative way that serves my highest good as well as the highest good of all those around me, free from any and all fears or doubts. I am my most authentic self, and I express myself fully as such to create a life I love. And so, it is.

"CONFIDENCE IS
10% HARD WORK
AND 90% DELUSION."

— *Tina Fey*

CHAPTER 13

DIRTY LAUNDRY AND THE BUSINESS OF TRANSFORMATION

"I don't even have the $175 dollars right now," she uttered in exasperation to me.

"My family put in the last of their $70,000 to get this food trailer up and running, and at this point, I'm not sure if it's going to last."

It was her response in regard to the registration fee for an event I was producing (a $10,000 food truck tasting contest).

I wanted her products to be something that people got to sample.

But when she told me "no," I didn't hear a real no — I heard a yes...with an excuse.

A wish.

A "that sounds good, but..."

So, I did not accept her rejection.

Because she wasn't rejecting my event as much as she was ACCEPTING her excuse as truth.

Also, something inside me told me that I wasn't going to leave there with a "no."

"Ok, look, I totally get it," I told her.

"I've had multiple businesses before and have wondered where the next dime is going to come from."

"Tell me about it!" she puffed in agreement.

I suggested an idea that might get her from a no to a yes.

"What if I threw in four hours of consulting with me to get to the bottom of how we can make your business more profitable?"

"SOLD! Where do I sign?!" she practically yelled as she waved her pen in the air.

I was overjoyed.

In hindsight it was probably because that was so cheap, but regardless, it was the first time I had actually sold "myself" in this way.

She was ecstatic, and we set our coaching meeting for later in the week.

When we met, she was going on and on about how she'd been through one employee after another, and how her current head chef was in essence taking advantage of her.

It was very clear to me that she had yet to take charge of her business.

In fact, she wasn't running a business.

Her business was running her.

She needed to fire those employees, knew it, and was afraid to do so.

But what is clear about others is rarely clear to us about ourselves.

This is where the saying, "You're always the last one to know" comes from.

Part of the dance of the business coaching/consulting that I do, is determining how much I can push a client until I create that light bulb moment for them, without ticking them off and having them storm off.

I am like the light switch, but they're going to be the one to choose to turn it on or not, so I get to figure out how to navigate the waters of their own curiosity — to move into a space of willingness to go beyond their fear.

In reality we're both dancing with fear.

I had to choose to not be afraid of what she'd think of me just as she needed to be brave despite what her employees would think of her.

Which is why I totally needed God, Universe, Spirit, Love, Light — whatever you want to call it — right there in that moment.

Bravery is always at our disposal if we're willing to take that first step and ask for it.

So, as I sat across from her, I thought to myself, "Dear God, WHAT does this woman need to hear right now? Help me give her the words that she needs."

And just a few seconds after my request, I got the words.

I actually got a picture.

It was a hamper full of dirty clothes, sitting in a corner of a room.

I took a deep breath.

"You know what?" I stopped her midway through her victim story.

"It's like you're staring at a pile of dirty laundry and expecting someone else to do it."

She kind of stared at me speechless for a few seconds.

"I can't believe you just said laundry" she mumbled with an air of shock and awe.

She continued, "I was looking at a pile of laundry just this morning and thought to myself that I can't do this anymore. That it's too much. That I can't handle a business and my life."

"Well," I said, "You've been handling it to a certain degree so far, and now it's time to do your own f*cking laundry and clean your business the f*ck up." (I tend to curse at appropriate times, in case you haven't noticed!)

After a few seconds I could see that she was finished being in the dark room and ready to flip that switch of light.

"OK, I'm ready," she declared, "Let's do this!"

She not only went on to fire those employees (I insisted she deal with it immediately and not put it off), but she took her business by the reigns.

It catapulted as a result.

And a couple of months later during the week of my event, two different news stations wanted a food trailer that was open early to be able to do a remote feed, so clearly, she came to the top of my mind.

And she got three spots on two TV stations for a total of six spots.

Not to mention the priceless value of taking her life and business back.

She has since gone on to launch her brick and mortar space, and now has a line of products at a major grocery store retailer.

Every time I see something in the news or something she's come up with, I am warm with the memories of how it all started and am honored to have played my tiny/major role.

Those moments were beyond magical.

That's the beauty of transformation.

It doesn't take years, months, weeks, days, or even four hours.

It takes an instant.

She became a new person.

She flipped that switch that I got to show her.

With one phrase.

One image.

Not from me, but THROUGH me.

Through my willingness to ask.

My willingness to listen.

And my willingness to speak.

That is the magic of our alignment when we tune into sacred orientation.

It's WAY cooler than we could ever imagine.

Mind blowing ecstasy...

Right there at a business meeting in a coffee shop.

No big deal...

And the biggest deal of all.

Just a typical day in paradise.

A paradise full of dirty laundry...and the business of transformation.

GIFT 13:
EMBRACE DOUBT AS ACCESS TO CONFIDENCE

There are a lot of universal truths I could pick out from this story, but the one that sticks out for me is my willingness to sell myself in the moment after she said no to the event I was originally selling to her. I could have just walked away. Plenty of people say no to the things I sell; if something isn't a fit, it isn't a fit. But I knew deep down she was a yes but was making excuses, so I continued to find something for her to say yes to.

Up until this time in my career, I had never really sold myself on a consulting level. One year previous to this I had attempted to start a mystery shopping service that failed because I did not believe in myself.

See, whenever we engage with someone, and attempt to "sell" whatever it is we're selling (no matter what the nature of the relationship is, or the topic at hand that we are trying to sell), people's objections are only tests to see how much you believe in what you're selling.

And that day I believed in me. I moved passed skepticism and into surety. To be clear and know my value. And because of that, ALL the other events happened. The magic, the connection, her taking on her business — all of it — because I moved past doubt and into confidence.

APPLICATION

Ask yourself, are there areas in your life where you are hiding and not being sure of yourself? Have there been times when you shrunk away into that doubt and lack of confidence? If so, what are they?

____

____

____

____

____

How would your life go if you held on to this way of being and continued your current course of actions?

____

____

____

____

What do you see happening if you chose to rewrite a new story?

____

____

____

____

INSPIRED ACTION:

I am going to ask you to meditate again. There is no right way to meditate. It's a practice, and the intention of it is to cause you to be still so that you reframe your relationship with your thoughts. Your mind will race, and that's kind of the point. You can focus on your breath, and you'll still drift. If you can make it an hour, that would be ideal, but really anything over ten minutes is a good start. It's bizarre that most people can sit for two hours for a movie yet cannot sit with just themselves for that long.

The point is to get you to feel that you are NOT your thoughts. You are the observer of them. More on this in Gary Zukav's, "Seat of the Soul." The more you see this and know that you are not your thoughts, the more likely you are to not listen to those thoughts of doubt that say you can't do, be, or say, whatever it is that you're wanting to express in the moment.

Meditation is a chance to both connect with yourself and break up with yourself. It's a daily practice that can only help you in your day-to-day life in your quest to be more confident and self-expressed, so set a timer, have a seat, and get to nothing!

After you have completed the action, take three deep breaths and repeat this phrase:

I accept the sacred orientation that is my knowing deep down. I acknowledge that I am loved and supported by the forces governing my universe, and I am a conduit of this love and support for myself and for others. I choose to love myself fully, to accept my past as part of my divine journey, and to forgive, appreciate, and embrace all the people, places, and things in my life as my access to that

divine love. I orient myself now to my truth, my power, and my love within, and I author my life in a co-creative way that serves my highest good as well as the highest good of all those around me, free from any and all fears or doubts. I am my most authentic self, and I express myself fully as such to create a life I love. And so, it is.

"TELL ME,
WHAT IS IT
YOU PLAN TO DO
WITH YOUR
ONE WILD
AND PRECIOUS LIFE?"

— *Mary Oliver*

CHAPTER 14

LITTLE BUTTONS, BIG DREAMS

"Hey dad, that's our house!" exclaimed my then 8-year-old son as he peered at pictures of my dream estate home displayed on my computer screen.

Currently apartment dwelling, he had caught me daydreaming/house hunting online, but he was more sure than I was of that house being ours someday.

"Oh yeah buddy?" I asked with hopeful curiosity. "What makes you say that?"

"Dad, just look at it. It has a gravity edge pool. And did you even notice it has a guest house? Grandma could totally live there. So yeah, it's our house."

"Well buddy, I suppose it could be. But if we're going to manifest that house, we're going to need a lot of forces of the universe working for us."

"Dad," he said with common sense declaration, "Are you forgetting? You ARE the universe."

(At this point I'm believing in reincarnation and that I have Gandhi 2.0).

"Wow buddy, you got me there! But first before we manifest that house, let's start with something small. My spiritual mentor says it's as easy to manifest a castle as it is a button -- the same principles apply -- so let's start with a button. Deal?"

"Okay" he says with an almost roll of an eye.

"Oh, wait, the rules!" I declare.

"What rules?" he blurts, now with full eye roll.

"Ok, so, we need to put some parameters on this button manifestation. First, it cannot be on any item of clothing. Second, we have to stumble upon it, no forced looking -- we're just going to allow it to appear. And third, it has to be before we go to bed tonight. Make sense?"

"Whatever," he says, clearly in a tune that acknowledges it's more my game than his.

"Do you believe you will receive the button?! Do you believe you have ALREADY received the button?!" I yell at the air as I take fruit out of the bowl on the counter to make breakfast, apparently like a pastor making an alter call.

"Why are you waving that banana around like a microphone?" Ben asked me, clearly convinced that his father was insane.

"Ok, fine, I'll calm down. Let's just go about our day."

And go about our day we did.

And we did.

And we did.

We visited our apartment office complex, grocery store, and then my daughter's day care to pick her up.

All the while my eyes were peeled for that button...to no avail.

Until our last stop to return a DVD to the pharmacy that also had a video rental kiosk outside.

Realizing that this was the LAST stop of the day and we were headed home after it (and already knowing that there were no buttons laying around the house), I was convinced that this was the last chance at manifesting that magical piece of plastic.

So clearly, I was not going to simply insert and return that DVD into that kiosk. I was going to SCOUR every inch of the machine, then the parking lot and everything in between.

"Where is that damn button?" I thought to myself in desperation. "I don't understand! It HAS to manifest! That's the ONLY way it can be! Why haven't I seen it?! Doesn't anyone care about the manifestation lessons I want to teach my children?!"

Clearly, I had forgotten about the rule about not looking for the button/it having to 'just appear,' and at this point I am exasperating both children, who were now wondering why their father was wandering the parking lot like a drunken idiot.

"Ugh, ok, fine, whatever...you win. I will receive the button when the time is ready for me to receive it" I exclaimed to 'the universe,' or whomever would listen to me.

In my mind, the button was no longer the button.

I made the button into the house.

I had decided that if I could manifest that button, that would mean that I could manifest that house, so all the significance of that house I attached to that fictitious button.

Even after I got home, I found myself looking into the cabinet a little bit more closely...you know...just in case.

“Oh my gosh, give it up you psycho!” I scolded to myself.

And not two seconds after that beautifully scripted self-deprecating thought, Ben stormed into my room, completely proud of himself.

“Look dad, I found it! The button!”

(Of course, leave it to my Mini-Gandhi)

“What?!” I exclaimed with almost-school-girl excitement.

“It’s actually two buttons, glued together, that I found in the fruit bowl,” he described. “We made it in school, and it was a wheel for some other craft. And I remembered seeing it in there.”

Not one button, but two.

DOUBLE what I asked for.

And the funny part is that it was in that fruit bowl I pulled the banana out of when I was making my faith declaration.

Seems I had a bit of a surrender journey to take that day instead.

And it was perfect.

As I concluded the day with my son (yes, the manifestation happened before bedtime), I got to reinforce the beautiful laws of the universe with him.

Ask and it is given.

Seek, and you shall find.

Knock, and the door shall be opened unto you.

Perfection.

It was over two years later that for Christmas he and his sister would give me a picture of them surrounded by buttons...with their names written in buttons as well, that I would realize life's true wealth:

They are my mansion.

Their love is my castle.

And their self-expression...is my dream come true.

GIFT 14:
EMBRACE ATTACHMENT AS ACCESS TO SURRENDER

I am convinced that one of the main reasons we're here is to experience love through the act of surrender. But HOW ATTACHED we can be. We can be attached to our ideas, our goals, our relationships, our things...the list goes on and on.

Sometimes it feels like we're wired for attachment. But the reality is, we're wired for surrender, and we're PROGRAMMED to be attached.

Look at your first nine months in utero. You're doing nothing. You're a process. All the nourishment you need is provided to you, and there is nothing for you to accomplish. It's all being accomplished for you. You are merely a space of allowing.

It is not until we get out into the world and start forming our sense of self (also called the ego) that we begin our attachment to that person/thing as a reality. And then we begin to relate to the ego as real. But it's not. It's an illusion we make up. And realizing that attachment to it can now give us access to know what surrender is, and to lean into surrender as a constant state of being.

For me in this story, the surrender wasn't even a full surrender either. There was still a large part of me that wanted that button when my son found it. But I had resigned myself to the divine timing of it and was leaning into the reality that I would not get what I wanted.

And then I was surprised.

Life is here to surprise us. It wants to sweep us off our feet! And that can only come when we surrender to the process of ALL of it. It takes practice, and it's totally worth it.

APPLICATION

Ask yourself, are there areas in your life where you are holding on to a belief that says you HAVE to have what you think you have to have?

How would your life go if you held on to this way of being and continued your current course of actions?

What do you see happening if you chose to rewrite a new story?

INSPIRED ACTION:

The thing that stood out to me was how my ex-wife gave me such a thoughtful Christmas gift, and how I shifted my mindset to be fully content with what I had in my children, even though I hadn't manifested that *particular* house I originally wanted. I moved into a space of happiness and peace, even though I didn't have what I THOUGHT I wanted. Yes, it was a joy that I actually manifested that button the way I did, but it was my child who manifested it, without any of my attachments. And then to receive that gift allowed me to see that I already had my dream house, right here, right now.

So, today's action is about setting an intention for something you want to manifest, declaring the parameters for it, and then surrendering to HOW it has to show up. You can write it down or declare it to yourself. Meditate on it and then let go of when or where it MUST come into your life experience. And then reflect on someone in your life that you can make a gift or card for. Even if it's just a thank you card, sending that "out" to the universe gives your desires that much more momentum. A physical card or gift is best too -- there's just something to gain from walking to a mailbox or post office that shifts our own internal energy into a space of gratitude, which is essential for surrender.

After you have completed the action, take three deep breaths and repeat this phrase:

I accept the sacred orientation that is my knowing deep down. I acknowledge that I am loved and supported by the forces governing my universe, and I am a conduit of this love and support for myself and for others. I choose to love myself fully, to accept my past as part of my divine journey, and to forgive, appreciate, and embrace all the people, places, and things in my life as my access to that divine love. I orient myself now to my truth, my power, and my love within, and I author my life in a co-creative way that serves my highest good as well as the highest good of all those around me, free from any and all fears or doubts. I am my most authentic self, and I express myself fully as such to create a life I love. And so, it is.

"I HAVE DECIDED
TO STICK WITH LOVE.
HATE IS TOO GREAT
A BURDEN TO BEAR."

— *Martin Luther King, Jr.*

CHAPTER 15

MEXICO & MAGIC DOLLARS

"Look, do you want to go or not? Because if you want to go, it'll happen, and we can go from there. But if you don't really want to go, it's just not going to work. So, the real question is really if you want to go or not."

As my business coach's words sunk into me, I felt my heart and the cells in my body react with, "Yes! Yes! Yes!" and at the same time my brain was saying, "No! No! No!"

It was an opportunity to spend a week at a secluded retreat destination in Mexico. We'd spend time diving deep into our old stories and moving past them. We'd eat a clean diet, journal on the beach, surf for empowerment, and do a whole bunch of other woo woo stuff around the fire at night, to and include yoga, meditation, and breath work.

Anyone committed to living their best life and moving to the next level would want to go; this is why my heart said yes.

And since it was an opportunity for me to move into a new way of being, all the old ways were going to duke it out to win, which meant they played a big "NO" game in my brain.

Some of the stories that carried out in my head were tried and true favorites:

"That's not even possible. How am I even going to come up with the money to get there, I can't even make rent?! I need to stop being so financially irresponsible. I'll never learn."

And last but not least, "I'm an idiot. I'm a loser. I'm a failure. I'm worthless."

It's funny the fiction that our brains come up with in order to keep us small and out of the big games that we are meant to play.

And the bigger the game, the louder the brain barks.

Freshly unemployed, yet whole heartedly into the work of developing myself inside dismantling the program that started the whole, "There's something wrong with me" conversation, I was not in a place to spend any extra money.

No credit cards, no wealthy aunts or uncles.

Borrowed to the max, running from the repo man, and living on the brink of evictions every other month, I was nowhere near the place of being able to do and travel wherever and however I wanted.

So clearly, I declared a resounding, "OK, let's do this!" to my coach.

I had to pay something to make my registration "for real," so I pretty much emptied my account with a $500 deposit to her, and the rest I was just going to trust to manifest.

And of course, within days the sh*t hit the fan...

On high speed.

My son got the flu.

I lost another consulting deal.

People stopped calling me back and ceased their business activity.

I didn't even have money for a plane ticket.

And still I pushed.

Even though I felt that it wasn't going to happen, I didn't utter the phrase, "I can't do this."

Instead, I asked myself, "How can I make this happen?"

This left the door open for it to actually happen.

It's like the saying, "Not if, but when."

So, guess what? No surprises, it happened.

Honestly, I cannot remember precisely how either. Maybe I sold something. Maybe I borrowed the money.

Like needing a life or death surgery, but feeling like it wasn't my body but my soul on the line, I just knew I needed to do whatever it took to be there.

So I got there.

And within a month of thinking I couldn't do it, I found myself meditating on a cliff among the ruins of Tulum.

Right there at one of the most beautiful places on the planet, broke as f*ck, and happier than I had been in years.

Perched on a rock, wind kissing my skin and sun warming my soul, I looked over at my coach.

She was standing there with eyes closed just soaking it all in.

She was by herself, which was odd — during the whole retreat she had been attended to by one person or another -- to find her on her own was a rarity, so I went up to her and declared my intention of income for when I returned stateside.

She stopped, looked at me, and put her hand on my heart.

I'll never forget it.

She said, "I just got a divine download. What if you did what we're doing here, but for people in the LGBT community? For people who want to overcome all their bullsh*t stories around their sexual expression. And you can do it just by being you."

Chills came to me then, as they come to me now, as that's what I'm creating, but not just for people in the LGBT+ community, but for anyone seeking greater self-expression and authenticity in their lives.

It was like all the cells in my body had been activated.

She knew it.

I knew it.

The seed of my destiny, planted.

I also need to remind you about that Christ on TV moment — do you remember the call out of DC I received in reference to Peter's miraculous catch of the fish?

He caught 153 fish, and ever since then it's been my "spirit number."

Every time I see a 153 out and about, I see them as little love notes from the universe that tell me I'm on the right and/or magical path.

Sidebar, we truly are ALWAYS right where we belong.

As I walked back from that cliff, COMPLETELY blissed out, I decided that I absolutely had to buy something for my kids while I was in Mexico, so I went into the gift shop located at the entrance of the park.

Determined not to be cheap with the $20 bill (almost all I had to my name at the time), I relished in the bliss of what had just happened, as well as who I was shopping for.

My amazing children.

It was all for them.

And they were for me.

I didn't get them much — some Mexican chocolate and a bracelet made by one of the locals — but it was my act of honoring them.

Honoring who they are.

Who I am.

Who we all are.

And as the cashier handed me my change, you know what I found?

A dollar bill that had 153 imprinted as the plate number.

Not as part of the serial number — the plate number — which prints MILLIONS of dollars.

I got in that moment how abundant life is.

How abundant I am.

And how abundant you are.

Anything less than that is a lie.

And anything less than magical is no way to live, no matter what we have or don't have.

Digits do not define us.

WE define us.

Our vision directs us.

Our orientation leads us.

Life gets to be a chance to NOT be governed by money, or any external force for that matter.

Life gets to be free from ALL constraints.

Because as long as money dictates our emotional way of being, we make money our god.

This is the gift of poverty.

This is the gift of Life.

A beautiful, bountiful existence.

It is infinite.

And so are we.

GIFT 15:
EMBRACE SCARCITY AS ACCESS TO ABUNDANCE

As long as money dictates our emotional way of being, we make money our god.

Wow, re-reading that still hits close to home. As you have seen, money has definitely played an integral part in my authenticity journey, and truth be told, the scarcity/abundance game goes on in one shape/way/form for me almost daily. Even writing this chapter I had to get complete and into integrity on what, if anything, I still owed my coaches. I found myself getting sucked into the emotion of it all. And, I feel that it's our journey to get money out of our way by pushing ourselves out of our comfort zones about making it our boss. And rather than fighting with it, learning to appreciate it.

Do we say we do things and the universe/money will support us? Or do we wait for support first before we do what we need and/or want to do? Recently I gave money to someone I do not agree with on a number of moral levels, but I did it as an offering/act of homage for my mother (it's a long story and I will have to save it for the next book), but what I got out of the experience was that we are at a pivotal time in our history where we are dismantling reality, particularly around the illusion of money.

Writing this chapter was great for me because I got to get complete on a number of my outstanding/nebulous agreements out there -- both for individuals I owe money to, and for individuals who owe me money.

It's just a piece of paper. A digit on the screen these days. A freaking pixel.

And we let it dictate how we feel, react, and live.

Well, this kind of reality does not work for me, so I get to rewrite it...daily!

Just like if we want results in the area of our bodies, we must move our bodies with intention on a consistent basis, we must also manage our money on a daily basis as to "show" the universe we are worthy to manage more.

And for me, the concept of embracing, and in this case embracing scarcity, boils down to releasing the resistance to it. We want to fight the scarcity because scarcity is bad. But really, we make it OK by acknowledging it, loving it, and then getting into action around creating more abundance. For if we fight being poor, we'll just live a life of arguing with ourselves indefinitely.

Again, this concept is a book in and of itself, and there are so many practices to be taken on in the world of abundant living, but what I want you to get out of this is to listen to your heart and say yes the next time you want to do something. Don't let a pixel stop you from doing whatever is on your heart to do, as I believe you are much more powerful than any pixel or piece of paper.

APPLICATION

Ask yourself, are there areas in your life where you are holding on to a belief that says you don't have money to do X, Y, or Z? If so, what are those areas?

____

____

____

____

____

How would your life go if you held on to this way of being and continued your current course of actions?

____

____

____

____

What do you see happening if you chose to rewrite a new story?

____

____

____

____

INSPIRED ACTION:

Today is a hybrid request. The first is to say yes to something or someone the next time you are asked. Say yes and see what opens up. Make sure your heart says yes too though. If you need assistance in understanding what your heart is saying, a good methodology is muscle testing. You stand up, tap your chest/clavicle a few times to reset the energy, close your eyes, and ask the question/declare an option. Your body will move forward at the most expansive idea, or shift backward if it's a, "No" for you. You can also do this by holding out one hand and pushing it down -- it falls down more at untruths or things of lower vibrations. Try it out!

The second thing I'm going to ask is that you make sure you're complete with your money if you're not already. Either getting complete with your debt picture, your monthly finances, or both. Have an uncomfortable conversation if you need to as well. Trust me, it'll hurt, and you WILL feel better after it. Create a spreadsheet of your expenses, and any/all money you make/will make/or owe. There are tons of free applications out there -- the point is to send the message to the universe that you are not being managed BY money, you are managing IT.

After you have completed the action, take three deep breaths and repeat this phrase:

I accept the sacred orientation that is my knowing deep down. I acknowledge that I am loved and supported by the forces governing my universe, and I am a conduit of this love and support for myself and for others. I choose to love myself fully, to accept my past as part of my divine journey, and to forgive, appreciate, and embrace all the people, places, and things in my life as my access to that divine love. I orient myself now to my truth, my power, and my love within, and I author my life in a co-creative way that serves my highest good as well as the highest good of all those around me, free from any and all fears or doubts. I am my most authentic self, and I express myself fully as such to create a life I love. And so, it is.

"WORK OUT YOUR OWN SALVATION. DO NOT DEPEND ON OTHERS."

— Buddha

CHAPTER 16

DEATH AND A TWEENAGER

"Dad, why did Uncle John have to die?" my freshly turned 11-year-old asked through tear-soaked cheeks as I attempted to tuck him into bed, barely a week after his great uncle had passed away from a terminal illness.

"Well, I don't know buddy. As your father I'd like to tell you a bunch of stuff to make you feel better, and at the same time, I feel like I can't do that. I don't know what I'm doing half the time anyway buddy. I'm making this up every day as I go."

"Yeah? So, what does that mean?" my sniffly boy continued to pry.

"Well, no one really knows anything," I confessed. "They just pretend to know. See, everyone just wants to feel better about being on earth and about dying. People will convince themselves of anything because death is a crappy thing to deal with. Some people believe in heaven, some people believe in past/future lives, some people believe in nothing. And it's all an attempt to be able to handle being alive, yet also living with the possibility that we can die at any moment."

"But I love you, I don't want to lose you ever," he pressed on, as the reality of death sunk in to his almost-teenager mind.

"Well, I don't want to be separated from you either. I don't even like to think about it. And at the same time, none of us is making it out of here alive. And that's the point. Because we don't know how long we'll be here, we let go of being upset...we choose to forgive...we love like there's no tomorrow. Because we don't have a guarantee that there is. We make every moment count, because the moment...THIS moment...is all we have."

At this point his tears had subsided as his brain and heart started churning.

He pondered my points and our conversation and came up with some of the most brilliant truths of humanity that a 'grown-up' could come up with, much less a child.

"You know what I think dad?"

"What's that buddy?" I commented, with genuine curiosity to hear what he had come up with the assuage himself.

"Well, I think that the earth is just one big recycling system. Like, there is NO WAY that a human could live forever, because the planet is only so big, you know? I mean, if every human lived forever, the earth would run out of food, water, land...all of it. So, humans have to die so that their bodies can be turned back to earth and whatever else the humans who come after them need."

Flabbergasted and inspired, the only response I could muster was a, "That makes total sense buddy."

"OR!" he exclaimed, "We're all just in a computer game. And we need to update our code for a new OS. It's not that the old code is BAD, it's just that it needs to go so that the new code can work and there won't be any errors when things get re-written. So, when people go, it's not so much about them, as it is about the code that needs to run for the new game to work after them."

At this point, I am considering building a shrine and alter to my tiny Gandhi/Buddha/spiritual prodigy that I have seemingly offsprung. I am moved to tears and warmth, as I realize that not only is he brilliant beyond words, but I also swell with pride in myself that I allowed him the space to explore his own truth.

To confront his own death as well as mine.

To be afraid.

To NOT know.

We gave a beautiful gift to each other that night, and it was a conversation that I'll never forget.

As I attempted to leave his room, he confronted me about my own grief he had witnessed in me.

"Oh, and dad? You know that sadness you have? You can recycle that into joy."

"It's done buddy. It's done. You did it just by who you are."

"But don't forget dad, it gets recycled because of who you are too."

"I won't forget buddy. I love you."

"Love you too daddy."

And I was complete.

GIFT 16:
EMBRACE DEATH AS ACCESS TO LIFE

Well, here it is, your answer to life -- reconciling death! OK, so maybe the answer to life is that there is no answer -- but in all honesty we spend so much of life grappling with death, or the idea of death, that we can actually miss out on the fact that life is not always meant to be taken seriously. "This beautiful sh*t show" is what I often call this life. The gift in death is that it gives us access to live fully.

What if we lived forever? There's a chance we'd do a whole bunch of things, but more than likely we'd get bored and end up doing nothing, and then end up in the paradigm we currently have! The fact that we don't know when it's our time to go enables us to live as if life is a full-time adventure, if we choose to see it as such.

Conversely, we can get hypnotized into thinking that we have all the time in the world, and we can PUT OFF doing what we really want to do. Ever thought about that person you'll break up with after the holidays? Yeah, there is no, "after the holidays." There is, and only ever will be, now.

This is the gift of death -- it wakes us up to be in the now. And this is being born again, and again, and again.

Regardless of your beliefs on what happens to us after we die, it is an inarguable fact that we are alive RIGHT NOW and making our lives better for ourselves and for those around us is a more than worthwhile pursuit.

APPLICATION

Ask yourself, are there areas in your life where you are holding on to a belief that says you have time to do what you want to do?

____

____

____

____

____

____

How would your life go if you held on to this way of being and continued your current course of actions?

____

____

____

____

____

____

What do you see happening if you chose to rewrite a new story?

____

____

____

____

INSPIRED ACTION:

This is a chance to get back into nature. I want you to find something to bury. It can be something as simple as a bean, a stick, or something of more value to you. It matters what it represents to you, and I want it to represent any low-vibration feelings you have. Grief, sadness, sorrow, resentments, any of it, I want you to put it into the ground. Doesn't have to be a big production but tell yourself that you're sending those things back to the earth where they came from. You can join them when you go back to the earth as well, but for you and your life RIGHT NOW, you will live without those things. You are recycling them into joy. Bonus points if you plant something new in its place!

After you have completed the action, take three deep breaths and repeat this phrase:

I accept the sacred orientation that is my knowing deep down. I acknowledge that I am loved and supported by the forces governing my universe, and I am a conduit of this love and support for myself and for others. I choose to love myself fully, to accept my past as part of my divine journey, and to forgive, appreciate, and embrace all the people, places, and things in my life as my access to that

divine love. I orient myself now to my truth, my power, and my love within, and I author my life in a co-creative way that serves my highest good as well as the highest good of all those around me, free from any and all fears or doubts. I am my most authentic self, and I express myself fully as such to create a life I love. And so, it is.

"YOU AREN'T YOUR WORK,
YOUR ACCOMPLISHMENTS,
YOUR POSSESSIONS,
YOUR HOME,
YOUR FAMILY...
YOUR ANYTHING.
YOU'RE A CREATION
OF YOUR SOURCE,
DRESSED IN A PHYSICAL
HUMAN BODY
INTENDED TO EXPERIENCE
AND ENJOY LIFE
ON EARTH."

— *Wayne Dyer*

CHAPTER 17

BLISS & THE BIG KAHUNA

"Oh, you must meet my neighbors. They're a gay couple and they're fabulous," my friend told me on the phone before I parked myself in her condo on the last leg of my couch surfing vacation in Hawaii.

Part of me wondered if she could hear the earthquake in my mind caused by how hard my eyes rolled into the back of my head.

It's something a lot of the straights think of us queer folks in the world.

Most of them think that just because two people are attracted to the same gender, they'll get along and/or be attracted to one another.

I hear it so much I don't pay too much attention to it anymore.

In hindsight, that's not the assumption she made at all.

At the time though, I had a lot of resistance to reaching out to her fabled yet fabulous neighbors.

But as I was about to leave her condo that day, I chose to knock on their door -- partly because I was curious who was home, but more because I wanted to get it over with.

And then he opened the door.

Saying that my breath was taken away isn't even close to the sensation that occurred when he made his appearance in front of me.

Caught somewhere between shock over my attraction to him, and that I was even having that kind of reaction, it took everything in me to muster what could be recognized as an intelligent sentence.

"Hi, I'm staying with Mags," I clumsily mumbled, "She said to stop by and say hi."

That's not even what she had said. I am already disgusted with myself for not keeping my sh*t authentic.

"Hi" he says, with a 'what else is there to say/how long might you stay at my door' air, although I'm also aware that this could just be my projection of my/his rejection.

We exchanged the usual pleasantries -- the weather, how long was I there, how long he'd been on the island, etc.

Then he tells me that he was born in the same hospital that I was born in on the island, separated only by four years.

I suppose this isn't too coincidental, but I lived 2,000 miles away and had not been back to the island in almost 40 years, so to run into someone who had been born where I was born seemed magically clandestine to me.

Even though he was partnered, and I didn't even live there, I found my mind (body) getting ahead of myself.

I both damn the obsessive gerbil of my thought brain, as well as make sure it gets enough water to stay in the wheel.

He asks me after a few minutes of chatting in the hall, "What are you doing right now? You want to come in? It's just me here."

Catapulted out of the gerbil wheel, I say with all the coolness I can generate as my heart started racing, "Are you sure? Okay," as if to answer my own question.

I am able to move past my self-disgust at the reality that I'm being allowed inside.

A beautifully quaint and comfortable studio apartment, it felt like the oracle's apartment from the movie, "The Matrix," mixed with its own Hawaiian character of surf and sand.

I meander through the kitchen, pass the bed, and make myself a spot on the couch.

I feel at home with the simple stillness.

A lazy Sunday for him, the last day of vacation for me.

I could have been anywhere that day, yet I found myself on his sofa.

And it was magical.

Throughout our conversation, I found myself wondering if I was just really attracted to him or if we knew each other in a past life.

Whatever it was, I felt intensely connected.

A combination of his essence mixed with the way he looked at me, I was impacted on a soul level at the presence of him being present.

I saw myself.

And I also felt seen.

"So, what's with your eye?" he inquired of my lazy eye with blunt yet kind honesty, the likes of which I was not accustomed to.

At this point I become hyper-aware of my poor eye contact -- before my surgery it was always there for me that I could not look people right in the eye and the presence of who I was left them questioning.

At the time though, it was a perfect opportunity for me to be with myself.

All that I was, and all that I wasn't.

I explained my medical condition, but shortly following that, he also comments on my dad shorts and my blockish feet.

"Who is this asshole?" I think to myself.

Deep down it makes me like him more because he just says whatever he wants.

We went on to discuss the role of religion and sexual conditioning.

Shame and sexuality.

It was a painful and beautiful conversation.

Our stories were so similar.

Me from the Southern Baptists, him from the Jehovah's Witnesses.

I was fully aware that as a society there is so much work left to be done, as well as fully present to the amount of work I have completed in myself that I am getting to witness in him, as my reflection.

The connection grows.

Totally fine with how life is at the moment, but also wondering if I hear wedding bells in the distance.

"Do you smoke?" he asks me as he gets up from the couch.

"Not anymore," I say sadly, as I feel our time together is coming to a close.

"Oh, because I was about to go downstairs and have a clove."

"Oh, cloves? I love cloves!"

All of a sudden, I'm a smoker now. I both love and hate myself.

It's about at this time that Mags makes her appearance, barging into my sacred space like she's on an episode of, "Friends."

"Hey guys, what's up?!"

I feel my eye roll transitioning to a death stare.

"Just like a woman to interrupt my hopes and dreams," I think to myself.

I answered curtly, hoping that she'd get the hint that now was not the time to do our nails and talk about boys.

Thankfully she picked up the "hints" I was dropping, as she left my soul mate and I to take our clove break in peace.

So, he and I headed outside, just blocks from the beach, had a clove (or two), and talked about love, life, and all the amazingly mundane things in between.

I was present to the same energy with him outside as when we were inside.

It wasn't his condo, it was him.

He was simply still.

I don't know if the cloves sealed the deal for me, but at this point in the story I was pretty convinced I was in the presence of a Christ.

"Maybe I was one of his disciples" I think to myself.

I quickly slap the schoolgirl inside, whipping her back into place as a reminder that SHE was a Christ just as much as he was.

Yes, he was a Christ, but not any more than I was a Christ.

This is the beauty of realizing we are all One.

The 82nd book of Psalms states, "Ye are gods, all of you."

Which clearly meant I had to explore whether or not I was going to fool around with either him or him and his partner.

Damn my testosterone.

We had exchanged a few looks here and there, and while I wasn't 100% sure that he was as into me as I was into him, I was fairly certain it was at least worth a shot.

Besides, I was on vacation, so what was there to lose?

I had never been with more than one person at a time. It's not that I was old fashioned or closed off to the idea, it's just that I hadn't had a burning desire to play in that way, so I had not actively pursued it.

That day though, I had to ask.

"So, I hope you don't mind me asking," while simultaneously not giving him any time to respond, "Do you and your partner have an open relationship?"

"Oh, we're not open," he says, in a way that shuts the door a whole lot less magically than he had opened it an hour or so before.

With an initial feeling of disappointment, it was in this moment that I realized how great he was.

And I moved into a space of gratitude.

I wasn't sad at all.

I was happy.

Happy that men like him still existed.

He was committed to his man in the way I wanted my future man to be committed to me.

In the way that I was already committed, to myself.

I got another level of understanding and clarity of who I wanted to spend my life with.

It wasn't just me.

It was whoever else wanted to play along in the meantime, with that same level of commitment.

It wasn't even about monogamy or polyamory either, it was about honoring their agreement to one another.

We hung out for a while longer...got homemade twinkies from a neighbor girl selling them on the corner, and I bought one for Mags as a peace offering for my bitchy behavior earlier in the day.

As he and I exited the elevator, we said our goodbyes in the hallway where it all started so shortly before.

Twinkies in hand, connections in heart.

It was simply perfection.

Once in Mag's condo, I had to catch her up on my fascination of him and how time stood still.

"THAT'S WHAT I WAS TRYING TO TELL YOU!" she screamed at me.

She must have felt that eye-roll earthquake after all.

She must also have forgiven me with my twinkie, because she declared that a celebratory swim at the beach was in order.

She and I talked incessantly about him as we made our way to the sea; you couldn't have wiped the bliss from our faces if you tried.

Getting to the shoreline, the wind on my skin and salt in the air welcomed me home.

I stepped into that water, and the cells in my body came alive.

Energized with passion, play, and purpose.

I was the water.

The force.

The flow.

Low tide.

High tide.

All of it.

It's not that I fell in love with that man that day.

I fell in love with who he represented.

Life wasn't about manifesting "the one."

Because I was already manifested.

I was "the one."

I fell in love with myself.

I fell in love with God.

And I fell in love with Life.

All that it was, and all that it wasn't.

Joy was no longer a possibility.

It was my reality.

Yes, I was alone, and I wasn't lonely.

I was connected.

One with all that was, is, and is to come.

I wasn't IN bliss.

I WAS bliss.

All the pain, all the crumbs along the way, all lead me to that point.

And I was complete.

GIFT 17:
EMBRACE DUALITY AS ACCESS TO BEING ONE

If you haven't gathered, this is the theme of this book. While I was going to share it at the conclusion, I feel it's appropriate to share it here because of how and why he and I connected. I asked myself what triggered our meeting? Personally, I do not believe in coincidences. I believe in synchronicities, and everything happening for a reason. Did our meeting occur because I made the commitment to follow my heart and get to Hawaii, even if it meant I had to forfeit a car payment to get me there? I mean, a call is a call, and I answer! Or was it my willingness to hear my friend and choose to knock on the door? My courage to knock on the door? Or maybe the fact that I was born in Hawaii and wanted to specifically go back to my homeland? How far back could I go to get to the "how" we ended up meeting?

Well, the answer is, that there is no clear answer.

We just met. And, I am choosing to believe that everything in our lives responds to the law of attraction, because we're all one big state of consciousness, just with different hemispheres.

It wasn't where I was born or any one thing I did to get me there, it was a culmination of all of the things. That magical instance was a byproduct of all the work I had done to live a life of authenticity, and I was a match to him because he had done the same.

Everyone, and I mean everyone, you meet or come into contact with, is a reflection of you.

The moment you drop the illusion of separation is the moment you begin to understand the verse, "Love your neighbor AS YOURSELF" in new and exciting ways.

It's not easy to drop the illusion, and it's totally worth it.

APPLICATION

Ask yourself, are there areas in your life where you are holding on to a belief that says we are separate individuals?

How would your life go if you held on to this belief?

What do you see happening if you chose to rewrite a new story?

INSPIRED ACTION:

Continue to incorporate meditation into your daily practice. It is by far the best thing you can do to break down the illusion of separation. But before you do, make a list of all the things you are grateful for -- both now and in the future. Let your meditation be one that's filled with the energy of appreciation. Feel that all of your life has shaped all of who you are. And all of everyone else is just the same.

After you have completed the action, take three deep breaths and repeat this phrase:

I accept the sacred orientation that is my knowing deep down. I acknowledge that I am loved and supported by the forces governing my universe, and I am a conduit of this love and support for myself and for others. I choose to love myself fully, to accept my past as part of my divine journey, and to forgive, appreciate, and embrace all the people, places, and things in my life as my access to that divine love. I orient myself now to my truth, my power, and my love within, and I author my life in a co-creative way that serves my highest good as well as the highest good of all those around me, free from any and all fears or doubts. I am my most authentic self, and I express myself fully as such to create a life I love. And so, it is.

"IF YOU JUDGE PEOPLE,
YOU LEAVE NO TIME
TO LOVE THEM."

— *Mother Teresa*

CHAPTER 18

A BIRTHDAY FOR THE BOOKS

"If I get an STD from an Episcopalian priest, I'm gonna be pissed!"

Those were my thoughts as I walked up to the red mustang rental car that had a license plate beginning with the letters STD.

Earlier that morning I had an uncomfortable feeling in my "down under", but I chalked it up to dehydration.

But three days before this I had spent my birthday...with a new, "special friend."

I had been in Hawaii for almost a week to celebrate my fortieth lap around the sun, and my first visit to my homeland since I left the island when I was four years old.

And other than this threat of a shameful infection, the vacation had been nothing short of amazing.

Waterfalls.

Snorkeling.

Hiking.

Sun gazing.

Kayaking.

Sleeping.

Meditating.

Exploring...exploring...exploring.

Meeting a soul mate and falling in love with myself.

And apparently at the end of the week I could add hooking-up to my vacation accomplishments.

It was my birthday after all, I deserved some fun, right?

Leave it to me to find the Episcopalian priest on a gay hook-up app.

In any event, we had a great, SAFE time believe it or not, but three days later as I checked in to my oceanfront lanai, the symptoms worsened, and I concluded:

That license plate was right.

“Figures,” I thought to myself.

I hadn’t had any kind of sex for months (not with anyone else at least), and the ONE TIME I get back on the court, this happens.

His text response when I told him: “Thanks for the heads up.”

The “heads up?”

Had this been where we had ended up?

Where I ended up?

Ironically, I was headed to a speaking engagement in Dallas later that week where I'd be speaking to a hospital restaurant association.

Speaking.

While carrying a shroud of silence.

Is it that some things are full of shame and we need to come out with it, or that some things are better left unsaid?

What's the line between painful secret and chosen privacy?

You rarely hear, "I'm just getting over a bout of gonorrhea, hooray!" touted on social media, but you'll see, "Down for the count with a flu," or "Home sick today."

Why is a sexually transmitted disease any different than a common cold?

In any event, I contemplated talking about it, and then it hit me:

The shame.

No one could know -- it was dirty.

I was dirty.

I DESERVED what I got because of my debauchery.

A sinner.

Dirty to the core.

And so was that priest.

My perfect reprobate mind delivered to me just days after my birthday.

But as I reflected more, here is what I came up with:

It was the SHAME that was causing the disease, not the other way around.

The shame was the shadow.

For those of us from religious upbringings, look at how much sexual shame we have grown up with.

"Masturbation is a sin!"

"Save yourself for marriage!"

"Stay PURE."

"Homosexuals go to hell."

Those were just some of the shame commonalities heard in the fundamentalist communities.

Being gay wasn't access to God -- it was a one-way ticket to eternal damnation.

And with plenty of disease reminders along the way.

This was the way I used to feel until I started learning that the body is just a feedback organism that relates to our beliefs and emotional states.

It was my belief that I was worthy of disease that gave the disease a place at the table.

We are the source of our own suffering.

Our own disease.

Our own hell.

I had a choice right then and there on that beach.

Was the shame going to cause a rift between God and me?

Or was the entirety of the experience an opportunity for access to the Divine?

Access to trust.

Access to surrender.

Access to UNCONDITIONAL love.

Well, I chose the latter, and didn't look back.

I've told a few friends along the way, and this is certainly the most public I've come out with it before.

But that's how we dismantle shame.

We talk about those things that we have been PROGRAMMED to be ashamed about.

Sex is not dirty.

Pleasure is not evil.

Homosexuals can even go to heaven.

Yes, diseases can happen, but it doesn't taint a person.

It makes them human.

Society is the one assigning stigmas, and the ONLY way we can dismantle those stigmas is by showing shame who the boss is.

By speaking our truth.

By owning our action.

And by living completely, wholeheartedly, and 100% out loud.

GIFT 18:
EMBRACE UNWORTHINESS AS ACCESS TO WORTHINESS

With every chapter I think to myself, "This is the most important gift to understand," but really...this is the most important gift to understand (until the next chapter of course). So much of what we accept or allow into our lives is based on our notion of what we think we are worthy of receiving. Actually, everything in our lives is based on the belief of what we are worthy of. Even saying, "I am not worthy to do this, that, or the other thing," is saying you're worthy to experience the opposite of it. Feeling unworthy to receive abundance is the same as feeling worthy to receive poverty. There are opposites sides to one coin, but it's all the same money.

The myth of making ourselves unworthy stems from a number of religions that establish a monarchical king and his servants. The belief systems promote humility to such a degree that we forget who we are (the Source) in the process of all of it. We buy into the idea that there's "poor little me" out there subject to the whims/fancies/judgments of some invisible judge in the sky, all the while neglecting to see that we ourselves are making the judgment. So even if there is a judge in the sky, we're still the judge saying so or not.

And it's this mindset that puts God out there, and us down here that can lead to a feeling of unworthiness to receive all the blessings that love ACTUALLY has in store for us. The irony is, declaring that you're unworthy is one of the most egotistical things you can do. Because it's in essence saying that of ALL the other beings and creatures of nature, it's YOU who doesn't deserve to be here.

No, you DO deserve to be here. We all do. And our task is to embrace all of life as perfect, whole, and complete...to drop the resistance that it be anything other than what it is, and to declare that we are worthy to receive all the beauty, truth, and love that we can contain. That we are worthy to receive a life BETTER than we can imagine.

APPLICATION

Ask yourself, are there areas in your life where you are holding on to a belief that says you're not worthy to be here? Or that you're unworthy to receive your heart's desire? And if so, what are they?

____

____

____

____

____

How would your life go if you held on to this way of being and continued your current course of actions?

____

____

____

____

What do you see happening if you chose to rewrite a new story?

____

____

____

____

INSPIRED ACTION:

Today we're going to get physical! If you have a physical condition that limits you in some way, you can skip it, but it's been proven that the physical action precedes the energetic feeling, so even if you don't feel like you're a champion worthy of greatness, standing for two minutes with your arms up in the air like you are the winner who is a champ, will make you feel like one. This is called a hero's pose, and I use it often. Do this today. Set a timer for two minutes. Smile while you're doing it. Declare that you're worthy of receiving your heart's desire. Bonus points if you read the daily affirmation while you do it too!

After you have completed the action, take three deep breaths and repeat this phrase:

I accept the sacred orientation that is my knowing deep down. I acknowledge that I am loved and supported by the forces governing my universe, and I am a conduit of this love and support for myself and for others. I choose to love myself fully, to accept my past as part of my divine journey, and to forgive, appreciate, and embrace all the people, places, and things in my life as my access to that divine love. I orient myself now to my truth, my power, and my love within, and I author my life in a co-creative way that serves my highest good as well as the highest good of all those around me, free from any and all fears or doubts. I am my most authentic self, and I express myself fully as such to create a life I love. And so, it is.

"TO BELIEVE
THAT YOU NEED
WHAT YOU DON'T HAVE
IS THE DEFINITION
OF INSANITY."

— *Byron Katie*

CHAPTER 19

TED TALKS & DELUSIONAL MUSTARD SEEDS

"Do you want to share your story? I'm producing a Ted talk event, and I'd love to have you be a presenter," my friend asked me as she sat across the table from me in an Austin coffee shop.

We had been chatting after a networking event that she and I both attended; come to find out she was producing a TEDx event that she wanted me to be a part of.

"Um, WHAT?!" I practically screamed, oblivious to the fact that we were in a coffee shop.

I was incredulous of what she asked, because I had just been rattling on and on about living authentic lives, attending breakthrough retreats, and doing my best to overcome whatever it was I was up to overcoming at the time.

She must have sensed my initial shock and confusion.

"Yeah, I love all of what you're saying, and I love the way you share it" she continued.

So, after my, “Um what,” I managed to eek out a, “Why yes, of course!”

I am a self-proclaimed Ted Talk junkie, so I did not take her words lightly.

And at the time I was completely obsessed with Breńe Brown (okay, still am), so the idea of being able to do anything like she did put me into full-on schoolgirl mode.

And no less than a day later, the panic set in.

Some of my doomsday thoughts were:

“What am I going to talk about?”

“Who am I even to be giving this talk?”

“I haven’t achieved enough.”

“This is going to suck.”

“I’m not worthy.”

“I have nothing worthwhile to share.”

“Other people have been and will be better than me.”

I went on and on.

Those are just a FEW of my “thoughtful friends” who shared their story.

As I began mulling over what I was going to say, I saw the beautiful irony in my story.

I WAS enough.

Period. Dot. The end.

My "story" was THAT.

That even "regular" people can be extraordinary.

And just to BE YOURSELF was enough.

As a human species, we find it so easy to compare ourselves to others, that rarely we step back and compare ourselves to OURSELVES.

The times are few and far between that we reflect and acknowledge ourselves for how far we have come.

For me, I had come so far in my willingness to be self-expressed.

And now I was coming from a closet of shame to a stage of light.

What an honor!

I understood in that moment, standing at my kitchen counter deliberating in my head what my topic was going to be, that it didn't matter so much what I had to say; it mattered more that I accepted the gift of the opportunity.

And bigger than that, the gift of existence itself.

The gift of me.

The gift of you.

The gift of life.

And with that, I came up with authentic momentum, dreaming big, and the talk that I'd get to deliver.

The big day finally came.

More excited than nervous, I found out the speaker order once I got there.

I was last.

I was going to shut — it — down.

I felt honored as well as pressured.

Which also meant that I got to pace backstage the entire time and miss half the show.

And it was perfect.

Not knowing what the other speakers were going to talk about, my talk ended up summarizing all their topics.

It didn't have the millions of YouTube views that Breńe's talk did, and that day was still pure magic for me.

I got to speak about the ways to bring our dream into existence by starting with our ways of being.

Our actions flow FROM our being, not the other way around.

When we are intentional with who we are being in the moment, and we bring our future selves into the present, the future we seek to create cannot help but manifest itself into the present moment one synchronistic instance after another.

From sitting in a coffee shop booth sharing myself to my friend, to standing on a stage spilling my guts, my dream had come true.

And it came from my commitment to my wellbeing.

By "being" my dream first, I acted from a place of allowance, trust, and surrender, and the physical material world flowed in to create my reality according to how I was. How I AM.

Causing our DREAM is about being who we'd be in the future, before the future has come to pass.

People who don't support me call it a delusion of grandeur.

And to a large extent, they're right.

Faith, does in fact, require an element of delusion.

Mustard seeds of insanity I'll call them.

We have to be sure of who we are and act accordingly -- despite the evidence to the contrary.

And, "acting as if" means we get to BE that future person in the present moment.

That is the reality of our D.R.E.A.M.

To Dare greatly, we get to be courageous *first*.

To Raise our vibration, we get to be joyful *first*.

To Embrace contrast, we get to be mindful *first*.

To Align ourselves, we get to be authentic *first*.

And to Move mountains, we get to be believing *first*.

This is trust.

This is surrender.

To accept it all.

And draw our destiny TO us.

Alan Watts calls this our wisdom of insecurity.

One day at a time...

One moment at a time...

One breath at a time...

So shall it be.

And it already is.

GIFT 19:
EMBRACE RESISTANCE AS ACCESS TO ACCEPTANCE

I hope you don't mind the redundancy and are beginning to see the pattern. We're creating new habits and new ways of being. And being fully self-expressed means accepting all of who you are, and all of how life works. And embracing all of that entails changing your relationship with resistance. We must stop resisting resistance! This means, you acknowledge when you're feeling stuck when you're feeling stuck. Affirm yourself no matter what. Love what's up. Fighting what you don't want will only get you a life of fights.

So if you want to live your dream, and have it mean something to both you and the world, the only way it will come to pass is if you truly take on that person who already has what you think you need. That's why I included the Byron Katie quote. As long as you relate to yourself as not having achieved X, Y, or Z, you will ALWAYS relate to yourself as someone who needs to achieve something first before you can be happy. And since there will ALWAYS be something to achieve, you'll never be happy.

Acceptance is about acknowledging all of what is so and moving into a future where you are fully self-expressed, free from any fear, doubt, or shame. And that can be done in an instant. A series of instances in fact, will create the life of your dreams.

APPLICATION

Ask yourself, are there areas in your life where you are holding on to a belief that says there is something wrong with the present you, something wrong with your present situation, or that you will have happiness after you get/achieve something that you don't have? If so, what areas/beliefs are they?

____

____

____

____

____

How would your life go if you held on to this way of being and continued your current course of actions?

____

____

____

____

What do you see happening if you chose to rewrite a new story?

____

____

____

____

INSPIRED ACTION:

Today's action involves the C word. Yes, commitment.

I'm going to ask you to commit to your dream, AND to commit to BE it first. Commit to BEING it, no matter what. Declaring it out loud works; writing it down is even better.

You commit to Daring greatly, so commit to being courageous first.

You commit to Raising your vibration, so commit to being joyful first.

You commit to Embracing contrast, so commit to being mindful first.

You commit to Aligning yourself, so commit to being authentic first.

And you commit to Moving mountains, so commit to believing first.

After you have completed the action, take three deep breaths and repeat this phrase:

I accept the sacred orientation that is my knowing deep down. I acknowledge that I am loved and supported by the forces governing my universe, and I am a conduit of this love and support for myself and for others. I choose to love myself fully, to accept my past as part of my divine journey, and to forgive, appreciate, and embrace all the people, places, and things in my life as my access to that divine love. I orient myself now to my truth, my power, and my love within, and I author my life in a co-creative way that serves my highest good as well as the highest good of all those around me, free from any and all fears or doubts. I am my most authentic self, and I express myself fully as such to create a life I love. And so, it is.

"FORGET THE PAIN,
MOCK THE PAIN,
REDUCE IT.
AND LAUGH."

— *Jim Carrey*

CHAPTER 20

DISTANT FATHERS & THE REBIRTH OF MASCULINITY

"Well, you do know that the acceptance of homosexuality is the precursor to the downfall of society, right?"

The words fell out of my father's mouth with little thought to who I was.

Who his own son was.

It was the Christmas of 2016.

I was 40 at the time, about 6 months after that magical trip to Hawaii, yet I found myself dropping into my old dynamic of how I acted around my dad when I was nine years old.

So, what followed my father's declaration that the apocalypse was nigh thanks to me and others like me, was us falling into more of the same of our usual patterns.

Me trying to get him to "see the light..." then him trying to get ME to "see the light..."

And do you know what was left over?

Darkness.

Emptiness.

Dissatisfaction.

Sadness.

I'm not sure when the desire for belonging starts as a child, but if we do not receive it from our primary caregiver, we can spend a lifetime trying to fill the gap.

My dad was a Marine, Southern Baptist pastor, and staunch conservative.

I understand exactly where his fear of accepting me comes from.

Not only was it from his misguided misinterpretation of the Bible, his fear of accepting me came from his own unwillingness to accept HIMSELF.

So, in that regard, I felt sympathy for him, and I had compassion rather than anger toward him.

I see this now because of the years I spent working on myself.

And yet, for years I held on to the notion that if I just tried a little harder, he'd love ALL of me.

He'd accept ALL of me.

He'd celebrate ALL of me.

Until that one eventful night in December.

I was finally done.

Done with expecting him to be ANYONE other than who he was.

Done with being attached to the idea that he would eventually change.

Done with wanting him to love me the way I loved my own kids.

And done with feeling so guilty about it all that I must continue a relationship with him.

See friend, we can still love our family and not have a relationship with them, and that is OK.

It's about setting boundaries that work for YOU.

But getting over our guilt that our present family is who they are, is what our journey is about.

On some level I like to think that there is a greater (unaware) part of my dad that agreed to play this role of cold and distant father so that I would understand the contrast of connection and love.

I get it now, because I didn't get it then.

And for that, the gratitude melts the guilt away.

But it was almost a year after this incident that the REAL miracle occurred.

I had reconciled being free from dad — I had always been the one to call but ended up making it through 12 months of missed holidays and birthdays without a peep from him.

I continued to pray for him and be grateful for him, but for all intents and purposes, he was dead to me.

And congruently my business had been failing to sustain me, and financially I was at my wit's end (again).

As a father, it's an extremely dark place to be when you cannot provide for your children.

At the end of my rope, I found myself at the same spot in my kitchen that my father had delivered his "eulogy" to me, yet this time I was on the phone with a friend, a man, who I greatly respected.

Not even three years my senior, he was already semi-retired from his Silicon Valley startup, sitting on the board of multiple charities, and even ran his own non-profit organization. A self-made millionaire, philanthropist, and father, I felt honored to know him, and continue to be inspired by his contributions.

We had shared many meetings and phone calls up until this point, but this one was particularly vulnerable, as I had grown tired of dancing with my financial shadows, and for all intents and purposes didn't care who knew about them.

And before I knew it, I found myself on the brink of tears, confessing my feelings on the matter, saying through an almost sob, "If it weren't for my kids, I just would not want to go on."

I am not sure what I expected at that point.

I didn't really care.

Apparently, I make spilling my guts an art form.

He replied with the most heartfelt opinion of me.

He told me that who I am...who I show up as...my expression, life, and my way of being, made a difference.

"The planet is better because of you," he told me.

He opened me to believe that my existence wasn't for my kids, it was for the world.

And I was a changed man forever.

He gave me what that little boy wanted so badly, and I didn't even know was missing.

It's like he took the sun and planted it in my heart.

I felt myself being flooded with light.

Shivers ran up and down my entire body, and my eyes started leaking uncontrollably.

I was reborn.

And all that was left over was lightness.

Fullness.

Satisfaction.

Joy.

See, in so many words, he didn't tell me anything I hadn't heard from my mother, but it was his father energy that healed me.

That which I defined as masculine — genuine power, love, contribution, success, vulnerability, openness, and connected expression — he had.

So, when he delivered the words, he delivered a gift.

And I was free.

In addition to his words of affirmation, he also offered me funds to keep the lights on before my job started — so he met my spiritual, as well as physical, needs.

I was beyond blessed.

I AM beyond blessed.

It started with me letting go of the things and relationships that no longer served me, followed by me really loving myself, and then the external world and its relationships eventually caught up.

They always do.

It takes time though — this is the way we want it.

For there is little satisfaction in a magic wand.

We want to do the work.

We want to let it go.

Because being reborn — is the experience of a lifetime.

GIFT 20:
EMBRACE REJECTION AS ACCESS TO RECONCILIATION

I don't know where along the line or to what degree you've experienced rejection. But if you're human, there's a guarantee that you've traversed those waters a time or twelve before. We all have that moment of feeling not good enough; it's more just a matter of how we handle those moments, and to what degree they are ingrained in our psyche.

For me, because the rejection was tied to my orientation, the wound ran especially deep, and took that much more time to heal. However, I believe that the key to my healing was through my accepting that I was rejected. Meaning, I did not reject my experience of rejection.

My father has actually passed away since I first wrote this chapter, and his passing inspired the final chapter of this book. Dealing with the father energy and forgiving my father has been one of the hardest and most rewarding tasks of my life. I actually understood how much of my daddy issues I put out onto "God" as well, as after I left the nest, my primary caregiver became invisible sky grandpa -- so reconciling myself through embracing the journey with my father actually enabled me to reconcile my relationship with that which I perceive God to be.

Through my self-love, I was able to then receive the physical love and validation that my friend gave me on that phone call. I had done the work first. Even though I was feeling desperate at the time, deep down I knew I was lovable and worthy to receive love, and it was such a blessing to experience such sweet reconciliation on so many levels. A beautiful journey indeed.

APPLICATION

Ask yourself, are there areas in your life where you are holding on to a belief that says you are rejected or worthy of rejection? If so, what are they?

____

____

____

____

____

____

How would your life go if you held on to this way of being and continued your current course of actions?

____

____

____

____

____

____

What do you see happening if you chose to rewrite a new story?

____

____

____

____

INSPIRED ACTION:

Today I want you to be that person who speaks value. Instead of looking for other people to act a certain way or say a certain thing, BE the change you wish to see in the world. Overcome the notion that there's anything rejection-able in you and tell a person in your life how special they are, how much they matter to you, and how much their existence matters in the world. You never know what they could be dealing with, and we receive by giving.

After you have completed the action, take three deep breaths and repeat this phrase:

I accept the sacred orientation that is my knowing deep down. I acknowledge that I am loved and supported by the forces governing my universe, and I am a conduit of this love and support for myself and for others. I choose to love myself fully, to accept my past as part of my divine journey, and to forgive, appreciate, and embrace all the people, places, and things in my life as my access to that divine love. I orient myself now to my truth, my power, and my love within, and I author my life in a co-creative way

that serves my highest good as well as the highest good of all those around me, free from any and all fears or doubts. I am my most authentic self, and I express myself fully as such to create a life I love. And so, it is.

"FOLKS ARE USUALLY ABOUT AS HAPPY AS THEY MAKE THEIR MINDS UP TO BE."

— *Abraham Lincoln*

CHAPTER 21

TWENTY DOLLARS & BEST DANCING DADS

You may feel like a lot of my "spiritual" stories are centered around money, and that's the way of so many of us who choose to come into this current space time reality.

Money makes the world go 'round, and money also isn't everything.

It dictates a lot of what we can and cannot do in life, and we get to decide to what extent our emotions are tied to our current economic situation.

Translated, the one thing money can never do (unless you let it) is to rob you of your joy.

True peace is found when you can be happy no matter what, and the choice is always up to you.

I'll never forget my daughter's first father/daughter dance.

It was the spring of her kindergarten year.

I had started a new job just shortly after my friend had lent me that money to keep the lights on, but I had not received my first paycheck and my account was down to an almost-negative balance.

Ignoring my car note, I bought my baby girl a corsage, which left me with less than $20 to my name.

This was her special night, and she was my special girl.

Damn my obligations, I was going to have a night to remember.

And...I am the one who will never forget it.

Her mom had been getting her ready, and I picked her up like her Prince Charming (poor or not, I was her everything that night).

She was as beautiful as ever, and even though I barely had a dime, I was honored to be her date for the evening.

It's funny how dads can put on their best faces for their daughters.

I knew that at some point she'd know the whole story.

But not tonight.

After we arrived at school, we made our way through the drug line, err, I mean, sugar line, and found our way to our spot at the cafeteria tables, now adorned with tablecloths, paper heart stencils and confetti sparkles.

As we finished our snacks and dinner (I had pizza, you know, for the children), I could hear the music coming from the gymnasium next door.

It was time to dance.

Despite the current lack-of-money story playing in my mind, I was going to love the present moment.

Some may call it delusional.

I call it magnificent.

My daughter practically skipped as we made our way from the cafeteria to the gym.

Sidebar, kids are just beyond adorable.

For all the bullsh*t we as parents deal with, they are totally, wholeheartedly, and completely worth it (insert swoon here).

OK, back to the story.

The gym was full of other daughters and dads.

Dresses and suits.

It was precious overload.

My money was irrelevant; I was in love.

The first song we heard was, "Shake it Off" by Taylor Swift.

It was perfection.

The lyrics and beat filled me as I literally began shaking it off... "but I keep cruising, can't stop moving, it's like I got this music, in my mind, sayin' it's gonna be alright..."

Let me tell you, I SHOOK IT OFF.

My daughter thought I was just being funny.

Little did she know I was being free.

Free from the stories of what it means to be a dad.

Free from the stories of what it means to have money.

And free from the stories of what it means to be a man.

Before I knew it, the PTA mom came over the loudspeaker and announced that the, "Daddy Dance Off" was coming up next.

She explained that a DJ would play a series of songs, and the PTA moms would pick off those dads who didn't have the moves.

In hindsight, they should have made a queer disclaimer.

Because ain't no straight dad stands a chance at me.

Now, I will say, once I started dancing, I thought I was either going to have a heart attack, die, or both.

But I was NOT going to lose.

Lord, men can be such competitive idiots.

Anyway, as they played the music, the moms began to pick off the dads one by one.

And before I knew it, it was down to me and one other dad.

Not gonna lie, he had some moves.

I found myself thinking, "Dang, I'm gonna have to do the worm to bring this guy down."

And not two seconds after that thought left the transom of my mind, HE dropped to the floor and started doing the worm!

"DAMMIT!" I thought, knee deep in sweat and heavy breathing.

"I'm gonna have to do a hand-plant now!"

So hand plant I did.

The gym went wild.

And down the other dad went (well, if you count the PTA mom picking him off as, "down.")

Before I knew it, they were declaring me, "The Best Dancing Dad" in the school.

The prize?

A $20 gift card to Target.

Good thing too, I wasn't sure where I was gonna get food the next day.

And now I did.

One more day done.

And one more night for the books (or, this book at least).

As my daughter and I left the school that night, I knew there was no other place I'd rather be.

No other girl I would rather take out.

And no other life I would rather live.

I was the best dancing dad, and I was in love.

GIFT 21:
EMBRACE BEING THE VICTIM AS ACCESS TO BEING VICTORIOUS

Here's another money story, but this one is rooted in the ideology that we can either be victims to our circumstances, or we can be victorious over them. I had every reason to be so stressed or anxious, but I chose to put my best face forward. This isn't faking it till I made it, it was realing it till I was feeling it. Like the hero pose, I chose to be happy and express myself as such, regardless of what my circumstances were dictating to me.

Being the victim has its roots in religion for me -- I got brownie points from sky grandpa if he saw me suffering. But at the end of the day I knew one thing: Suffering no longer worked for me, especially if an invisible force had the say. Embracing that I am victorious comes from embracing that I have something to become victorious from, and in this case, it was victory over victimhood...by way of a handplant.

APPLICATION

Ask yourself, are there areas in your life where you are holding on to a belief that says you can't express joy? If so, what areas or beliefs are they?

How would your life go if you held on to this way of being and continued your current course of actions?

What do you see happening if you chose to rewrite a new story?

INSPIRED ACTION:

Twenty something chapters in and FINALLY we get to dance! I didn't mention the one time I went to a club by myself and started dancing on my own...sober...but if you really want to get out there, do that! But bare minimum, dance at your house...regardless of how you feel. It's even more imperative to do so if you don't feel like it! There are lots of dance playlists on YouTube or Spotify or the like, but you know what makes you feel good. A good idea is to pick music from a time in your life that makes you feel good. My current favorite is, "Good Time to Be Alive" by Andy Grammar, but you do you! Also, bonus points if you take a Wi-Fi speaker outside and do a dance run someplace public!

After you have completed the action, take three deep breaths and repeat this phrase:

I accept the sacred orientation that is my knowing deep down. I acknowledge that I am loved and supported by the forces governing my universe, and I am a conduit of this love and support for myself and for others. I choose to love myself fully, to accept my past as part of my divine journey, and to forgive, appreciate, and embrace all the people, places, and things in my life as my access to that divine love. I orient myself now to my truth, my power, and my love within, and I author my life in a co-creative way that serves my highest good as well as the highest good of all those around me, free from any and all fears or doubts. I am my most authentic self, and I express myself fully as such to create a life I love. And so, it is.

“TURN YOUR
WOUNDS
INTO WISDOM.”

— Oprah Winfrey

CHAPTER 22

DIRTY DISHES, TINY SHAMANS

"Dad, I kinda don't want my friends to know you're gay."

My son's words escaped him with an air of a timid confession.

I remember looking into his eyes and seeing innocence blended with an air of fear.

Ignorance sprinkled with a bit of shame.

Barely eight at the time, his words sunk into me and hit me at the core of who I was as a father.

I understand that I will not be able to shield my children from pain, and at the same time the absolute last thing I want to do is to be the cause of their pain.

In that moment I felt like I was the source of his pain.

So, what did I do?

What I normally did.

Buried it.

Internalized it.

Made friends with my shame...this time masked as my son.

Now, I didn't carry the shame in the same way that I did when I was completely in the closet.

But that's the thing about shame.

It's subtle.

We justify it.

We spend so much time with it that we think it's a normal way to be.

Our children understand what life is and who they are based on our example, and at the same time they give us access to who we are based on their example.

They come out of the womb completely free from shame, ready to show us bliss in the moment and the joy of the human experience.

They don't get shame from themselves; they get it from us.

To know this fact is the most beautiful and painful gift I can imagine.

Even with this understanding, shame can hit us like a ton of bricks, and the last thing we as parents want to process is the idea that our children are ashamed of us to the degree that it's causing them pain.

Since my response was to shut down, I don't even remember what my reply to him was at that time, because I did not process it until a fight we'd have three years later.

Three years.

It was any normal school night.

Rushing around. Love. Bickering. Hugs. Homework. Chores. Dinner. Dishes.

Etc., and repeat.

But deep down I was tired.

Not just physically but mentally and spiritually as well.

At the brink of feeling like I was living someone else's life, I found myself checked out yet again, and going through the motions with just barely enough wherewithal to keep the kids from murdering each other.

After dinner, I asked the kids to do their own dishes.

They had been arguing with each other already, so my fuse was shorter than normal.

In response to my request for his compliance (aka, demand for obedience), my son proceeded to thrash his dish in the sink with his signature rebellious way of gesturing and eye rolling.

A perfect reflection of my stubborn independence, he knows exactly how to push my buttons.

Before either of us knew it, water splashed onto the floor and then on to my computer.

It was a few drops (I'm typing on that computer now, clearly the world is still turning), but that was all it took.

The dish was put down, and the last straw had been drawn.

I was done.

"DAMMIT BEN! WHAT THE HELL?!" I screamed with three years' worth of fury.

"JUST GO. JUST GET TO YOUR ROOM. GO TO YOUR ROOM! JUST GO!"

His stunned silence spoke volumes.

He attempted to speak, and I cut him off with yet another holler, "JUST GO!"

Disgust for myself filled me as I proceeded to clean up the spill after he left.

"I've scarred him for life," I said to myself as I began to step into the what-if-whirlpool of utter parental failure.

"I can't do this...this is too hard...where did I go wrong... how can I make this right...and I may just give up," were just a few dark passenger thoughts in that tempest of my mind's self-destruction.

I collapsed to the kitchen floor, sobbing with sadness and exhaustion.

"Is this it?"

"Is this my life now?"

"I scream at my children?"

"I'm THAT dad?"

I let myself cry there for who knows how long, and somehow, I managed to peel myself from the cheap laminate flooring in my rental home, which further triggered my hatred for the moment.

But deep down I knew I had to get up.

Getting up is the only thing we can do sometimes.

And THAT is enough.

They say not to go to bed angry, so I made my way up to his room to apologize, but I kept it short and sweet.

I wanted to talk to him more, but I was just processing way too much anger.

At him.

At myself.

At life.

Triggered by a damn dirty dish.

It wasn't until later that night that I saw exactly what I had been doing.

The lightbulb moment went off when I was in the shower.

I had been projecting all my shame onto him.

His shame was a reflection of my shame.

I had been limiting love from my life and telling myself it was on account of the children.

Sure, I experienced a lot of love, but I was blocking capital L-Love.

Deep love.

For him.

For myself.

For life.

From that time he told me that he didn't want his friends to know I was gay, I was telling myself that I was just putting off a relationship until after he was older, but deep down I still wanted a relationship, so I was blaming HIM for MY choice.

"Oh my God, I'm an even sh*ttier parent than I thought I was!" I thought to myself as the hot water hit my face.

"Wow, wow, wow," were the only words I could think to myself as I finished getting ready for bed.

I made my resolve to offer him a proper apology the next day.

And not just for screaming at him, but for projecting all my anger onto him and making him pay for it.

After school the next day I found myself in my room with nothing but the space to speak to him and to take responsibility for what I had been doing for over three years.

The words stuck in my chest, then constricted my throat.

"It's now or never," my insane brain prodded in tandem with my heart.

“Hey buddy,” I squeaked.

“Yeah dad?”

“So, there’s something I need to confess.”

“Yeah?” he said, now piqued by curiosity.

“Well, remember that time you were in 3rd grade and you said you didn’t want your friends to know I was gay?”

“What? I didn’t say that!”

“Well bud, you did, I remember it like it was yesterday.”

“No way, I don’t even remember that. Besides, it doesn’t matter, that’s not even true. I don’t think that.”

“Really?” I said with half-belief.

“Yeah, really,” he continued, as if to signal the notion that I had been the instigator of all this made-up drama in the first place.

“Well, here’s the deal buddy. I don’t want to be the source of your pain, and at the same time, nine times out of ten, kids are going to find something to make fun of each other about. I want a relationship and think I’d make a great partner. I am ok to be without one, and at the same time I don’t want to push one away on account of thinking it will protect you from getting made fun of. I made a choice to push love away and I blamed you for it. And for that I am deeply sorry. Do you forgive me?”

“Yeah dad. Of course!” he said, completely oblivious to my inner turmoil.

Kids are so damn resilient.

“I love you buddy. So much.”

He declared, “Love you too dad” as we hugged, and he left the room to leave me with my joy and relief.

What occurred that day was just one of the times the children have led me to the road of a deeper self-love.

He carried my shame because I put it there, and now he gave me forgiveness because of his own mercy.

And because of HIS self-love for who he is.

He gets it (and I’m pretty sure I do as well, leaving room for my consistent error of course).

Months later I would find myself in the kitchen just giving him some love and asking him, “Hey boo, do you love YOURSELF more than you love me?”

A “Yes” slipped out of his mouth almost a little too quickly, leaving me a bit shocked as well as proud.

He continued, “But that means you have to love yourself more than you love me Dad. Do you love yourself more than you love me?”

Glee filled my body as warmth and chills filled my veins.

“I’m getting there boo, and yes, thank you. As much as I like the idea of us loving each other the most, the relationship that we have for ourselves is the only one that’s guaranteed to last as long as we live, so we are worth it!”

He agreed, but I think just to get me to move so he could get ice cream out of the freezer.

Later that night I heard a song that I took as yet another sign from the universe.

The lyrics went on, "Love yourself as much as I love you."

The signs have been all around me.

And are all around all of us.

This entire journey has been about reconciling my relationship with myself.

To love myself.

I am it.

My own perfectly imperfect companion.

It's not about me finding "the one."

I am the one.

I'm done.

And at the same time, I am just beginning.

Because now it's YOUR turn.

Single or not, YOU are your own perfect partner, because you're gonna live with you for the rest of your life, guaranteed.

This was the gift of my children and can be the gift of ANY of the people in our lives.

To shine our light.

To release the shame.

To embrace our shadow.

To love what is.

And to finally love our Life.

Dirty dishes and all.

These are my tiny shamans.

Living in my house...

While leading me home.

So may they lead you home now as well.

And may you find your love within.

GIFT 22:
EMBRACE JUDGMENT AS ACCESS TO APPROVAL

Shame, judgment, and rejection, all play a dance with honor, approval and acceptance. They're all kind of just like different flavors of the same ice cream. By this time, I hope you're seeing that there is no shame other than what you agree to take on, and there is no judgment other than that which you determine is accurate. On some level the naive fear of my child to not get made fun of, triggered my own internal shame and judgment. But it was my willingness to acknowledge my shortcomings, to be with them/process them, and get up off the floor that brought about what I feel is the miracle of approval.

Only we can determine if we are approved/good enough. Only we can give ourselves permission to be happy. And only we can allow our own freedom. As Oprah says, our wounds indeed lead to our wisdom, so let your wisdom arise from the floor of your sadness. May you drop the judgment of yourself and may you approve of yourself right here, right now.

APPLICATION

Ask yourself, are there areas in your life where you are holding on to a belief that says you've done something that's worthy to be judged? If so, what are they, and what would it take for you to feel approved?

____

____

____

____

____

____

How would your life go if you held on to this way of being and continued your current course of actions?

____

____

What do you see happening if you chose to rewrite a new story?

INSPIRED ACTION:

Today is another nature day. I want you to get out and have a walking meditation. If you are unable to walk, make it an outdoor meditation. The point is to get into the cycle of the earth. Walk for at least ten minutes, taking deep breaths in an out as you do. Notice the rhythm of the earth. Feel yourself sync to the process. Realize that there is no judgment. The only one who can judge you is you. The only one who can grant your approval is you. And it's not later. It's now. Feel your arms and legs swing with the motion of the coming and going of life. The trees, the sun, the wind. It's all you, and it's all us. Acknowledge yourself for coming this far, release any judgements you've held toward others or yourself on the journey, and exhale any shame that may be left. Get complete and have a conversation with anyone if you get a picture of them during your walk. However you get complete is up to you.

After you have completed the action, take three deep breaths and repeat this phrase:

I accept the sacred orientation that is my knowing deep down. I acknowledge that I am loved and supported by the forces governing my universe, and I am a conduit of this love and support for myself and for others. I choose to love myself fully, to accept my past as part of my divine journey, and to forgive, appreciate, and embrace all the people, places, and things in my life as my access to that divine love. I orient myself now to my truth, my power, and my love within, and I author my life in a co-creative way that serves my highest good as well as the highest good of all those around me, free from any and all fears or doubts. I am my most authentic self, and I express myself fully as such to create a life I love. And so, it is.

"IT'S KIND OF FUN
TO DO THE IMPOSSIBLE."

— *Walt Disney*

CHAPTER 23

GURUS, GOD, AND ALCOHOL

I was two days into a "New Year, New You" Facebook group online event.

It was a seven-day journey, with assignments each day.

The first day we were to write down our vision for what we wanted to see manifest for the year.

And on the second day, we got to write all the ways we'd screw it up.

All the shadows, demons, dark passengers and saboteurs, right there in front of me in black and white.

I had pages.

Good news though, we got to burn the list when we were done, as a means to transmute their energy.

Congruently (and unrelated to the Facebook group), I had felt led to a personal development seminar down in Orlando.

I had to MOVE MOUNTAINS to get there (again, apparently how I roll), and once I was there it was a great reminder to me that, yes, I can do anything I set my mind to (and a great reminder of how supported I am).

I went to the first day of the seminar, and by the end of it I was pretty mentally spent, as well as physically hungry.

The only thing within walking distance was an Applebee's, and for me, that was good enough (please don't take away my gay card).

The organization producing the event had an agreement that we not consume alcohol or drugs during the week, as it would affect the level of deep consciousness work.

However, I took it as a suggestion.

Traveling, without my kids, drinking is what I did.

So even if it was crappy wine at an Applebee's, I was going to treat myself (hooray, gay card redeemed).

Within an hour or so I had made besties with the other alcoholics at the bar, and in no time at all I was sharing myself and getting them to open up.

Before too long I started talking about my notebook assignment and all the ways I'd screw up 2018, and then I brought it out with me and started reading it.

"What?! Dude! You really think that?!" one of my new best friends exclaimed to me.

"Oh yeah, but I mean, I don't BELIEVE those thoughts though. We all have crazy ideas that we'll mess things up,

I am just OK with the voices enough to be able to share them, as they don't have power over me."

"Wow man, that's crazy." (at this point he was lit enough to think anything could have been crazy).

I suddenly realized my overdue task and roared a little too much for public, "Oh my gosh, I have to burn this, I was supposed to do it yesterday!"

"Oh, I have a lighter!" one of the others squealed with glee.

It was a yellow lighter with "YAAAASSSSS" emblazoned with hot pink letters.

It was perfect.

Perfect for me.

Perfect for the moment.

Perfect. Perfect. Perfect.

I told them I'd be right back.

And so, my negative energy was ceremoniously cleansed right there in the Applebee's courtyard.

I even took a video and uploaded it to that Facebook group.

I felt like Tom Hanks in Castaway as I declared, "I...Have made...Fire!"

I made my way back from my tribal ritual of one, got the others caught up to speed, and before I knew it, they were buying me shots alongside some other Floridian rum drink.

It would have been rude for me to say no, right? Plus, I was Ubering home, so it didn't land for me as irresponsible.

Until the next morning, err, I mean, later that "night."

I got maybe 4 hours of sleep, when my body woke me up in an extreme state of grossness.

I wasn't nauseated but felt completely off.

Dizzy with my own disgust.

Hungry, tired, but also not able to sleep, I walked myself to the nearest McDonald's as I contemplated existence.

A few years back, I committed to "go sober" for a year, which I did — mainly again to prove to myself that I could do anything I set my mind to.

It was very empowering, and at the same time I related to the experience like alcohol was something I was missing.

So, I concluded my year and went back to drinking occasionally or socially, telling myself that I was only having a couple of glasses of wine a night, which was vastly different from the six-pack of beer and bottle of wine a night I consumed in my restaurant owner/closeted days.

But even though I didn't consume as much as I had previously, I would still find myself getting drunk at least a few times a year, this night being one of them.

As I got back from feeding myself and taking a shower, I really wondered if I'd ever be able to have a balance.

To be "normal."

It was clear that something was off, but I wasn't clear what.

However, I knew I could at least commit to not drink any more that week, especially because that's what the conference organizers had asked anyway.

"OK, a week. I can do that no problem," I thought as I finished getting ready.

I started packing my briefcase to head to the conference center when I noticed my notebook on the floor.

Just a few short hours before being so amazingly authentic with my new alcoholic soul mates, I flipped it open and noticed the first page was still intact.

Apparently, I neglected to rip that one out and burn it with the rest of the others.

And I saw it right there, in more black and white truth than ever before.

On the top of the line of how I'd screw up the year — the very first line:

I'd get too drunk.

WOW. WOW. WOW!

I had gotten too drunk to even complete my task of how I'd not screw up the year, because deep down I feared that I'd get too drunk.

Talk about an immediate self-fulfilling prophecy!

It was at this point that I was convinced that the greater part of me, God, whatever you want to call it, is a hilarious and brilliant force.

It was just too perfect, painful, and downright funny as hell.

I felt done with alcohol after that day.

I quickly told my Airbnb host all this information and asked him for a lighter to burn that last page.

He was like, "Hey man, that's cool! I gotta burn some sh*t too!"

I felt inspired and energized.

Later that morning, I came clean with my Facebook group as well as the conference leaders.

As we got into the second day's material, something else began to feel out of alignment.

They started selling their "next best thing," and elevated their leader by only showing video of him, saying that if you wanted to see him you had to register/buy the next thing.

"It's like humans have lost the script on how to live. And we have that script" he declared from a screen that all the attendees were staring at.

I could go on, but it was clear that I was out of alignment by being there, and it was time for me to leave.

I knew that if I was to have any conversation with the leaders about it that they'd turn it into my resistance that I needed to work through.

So intoxicated with their own transformation Kool-Aid, they wouldn't tolerate any reality that one can learn and grow apart from their organization.

It all became clear just how done I was.

See, I was more than just addicted to alcohol.

I was addicted to my thoughts.

A functioning workaholic and alcoholic, addicted to figuring it out.

Just one more seminar, class, or retreat.

Just this one more self-hep book, YouTube video, or life coach podcast episode, and I would be fixed.

Now here's the deal, the work I have done on myself has been extremely transformative and beyond helpful.

I have done things and created things that the average human wouldn't dream of.

I have done the WORK.

But it can get like therapy — there is a time when it's needed a lot, and hopefully a time when it's needed for maintenance.

When I was first coming out, experiencing foreclosure, bankruptcy, and divorce, I needed support.

It was like I had a broken bone and "the work" was my cast.

But it got to the point where the bone was healed, and I was keeping the cast on.

The cast then became the problem — weakening the bone and rotting the skin.

So, as I left the conference center and practically ran toward my escape vehicle, I envisioned breaking that cast and running on my own.

It was time for the student to be the teacher.

They were not my gurus.

I was my own guru.

Not as if I had all the answers, but just to inspire others to find their own.

I don't have the script for how to live your life — only you have that.

We are ALL gurus.

Since I left the conference before it was over, I got home and was completely surprised how my desire for alcohol was almost non-existent.

It was as if my cells constricted at the thought.

My body AND brain said no, for the first time EVER.

No longer was I feeling like I was missing anything.

All I wanted was to hydrate, hydrate, and hydrate.

And there was no more mental chatter either.

Between this and the little/huge occurrence of the notebook situation, I was convinced that God was NOT actually out to get me.

What a sweet gift, yes?

Still though, with all of that, it was only three months later that I relapsed, and I'd find myself drunk yet again — this time a choice (rather than a craving).

It was clear that I didn't crave it.

It was clear that I didn't need it.

And it was clear that I was still choosing it and finding myself back in the mental masturbation of how to find a balance.

When I had committed to a year previously, that was just a year.

Coming back from Florida, committing to a whole lifetime felt sad at the time, so I committed to one day at a time.

After a while of not having it, it led me back to thinking I could handle it.

I believe we're up to illusion #3,457 at this point, yes?

So yet again, I was at what I'd consider to be my final crossroad between alcohol and me.

I told myself I could be the alcoholic sage — the old man who had his whiskey every night.

I told myself I wasn't consuming that much, that it wasn't that bad, I was exaggerating, and that I could handle a "normal" amount of consumption and have a "normal" kind of life.

I told myself I'd do it after such and such holiday, party, or wedding.

I told myself all the things I always do to keep my juice where I thought I needed it.

God had given me a gift and I was crapping on it.

Turns out me, the strong guy — the "can do anything" guy — actually had a weakness.

A weakness that relied on that invisible guru in the sky — that force of Love and mystery that keeps our hearts beating and this ball of mud suspended in mid-air, floating about in the middle of nowhere.

That mystery had my back.

We were co-gurus.

So, we made a deal and I said goodbye to the juice forever.

I've made it a year; I can make it a lifetime.

I may lose some friends, and I'll gain some new ones.

I am also processing resistance to this declaration, writing this chapter and posting on social media to hold me to account.

That's part of why I am here though — to be SO ok with life being a bit of a mess, and authentically sharing it as such, that it inspires you to be more ok with yourself and express yourself authentically as such as well.

Life is not always about succeeding at the thing and then sharing about it afterwards.

Life is about sharing about the thing and succeeding through success OR perceived "failure."

It's about learning, loving, laughing, and growing.

It's about honoring what works for you.

All of us have vices to work through, accept, and then dance with.

I am writing this on a plane, on my way to a wedding.

And we all know what you do at weddings — YOU DANCE!

See, we can make life what we are missing out on, or we can make it what we get to experience, which is love, love, and more love.

Life is what we make it, no matter what.

It's about finding our truth and honoring it.

It's about falling down and getting back up.

It's about giving our best, no matter what.

It's about accepting the love, grace, and forgiveness that's been there for us all along.

It's not in another person, substance, place, bottle, or thing.

It's in you.

Strength as well as weakness.

God in us.

So, raise a glass of awesome with me, and cheer this amazing life.

Your inner guru will thank you for it.

And so will I.

GIFT 23:
EMBRACE YOUR MESS AS ACCESS TO YOUR MESSAGE

A lot of the times we refuse to think our lives are anything special. That we're all a little bit messed up. But let me tell you something, we are at a crucial time of evolution for our species. There is so much hurt and pain in the world, and there are also rapid amounts of healing and conscious awakening. Just look at how much more mainstream yoga has become. And that practice is all about union with God through our breath. Even if you don't believe that, the practice brings forth more health as well as healthier mindsets. We are at a time when our work is clear: we have a bit of a mess to clean up.

Which is where our message comes in. My mess was a life of inauthenticity, shame, guilt, and self-hatred. I've turned it into my message through my willingness to share it. Others have told me it inspires them to be more brave, courageous, and "out there." This, in turn, inspires those they know (people I do not know) to do the same.

And that's just little old me. I'm thoroughly convinced that we're on the crest of a tsunami wave of transformation, and the more of us who embrace our message as a GIFT -- as a MESSAGE of hope, healing, and redemption, the more peaceful and productive our lives can be. It's about taking personal responsibility, owning YOUR story, and showing as the only you in the universe...because you are!

APPLICATION

Ask yourself, are there areas in your life where you are holding on to a belief that says your message isn't pretty or packaged enough to share? If so, what are they? Write a book if you need the room to explain!

____

____

____

____

How would your life go if you held on to this way of being and continued your current course of actions?

____

____

____

____

What do you see happening if you chose to rewrite a new story?

____

____

____

____

INSPIRED ACTION:

Well clearly, you're going to write a list and burn it or flush it! In the beginning of the book you made a list of resentments to destroy/transmute. Now you're going to destroy/transmute any remaining negative stories that you're currently making up. I call these memes -- they are simply negative thought creations created to dictate a reality. They'll say things like you can't do this, that, or the other thing. They'll say you're too ____________ (old, young, skinny, fat) or whatever else to be able to do it. The list could go on and on. Remember I had five or six pages. Maybe yours is that you'll get too drunk too. Who knows? The point is, you're going to burn that list and make a new one. After you've destroyed it, make a list of all the positives in your life, as well as all the things you want to do, and especially the list of people who can be helped because you were able to transmute your mess into your message.

After you have completed the action, take three deep breaths and repeat this phrase:

I accept the sacred orientation that is my knowing deep down. I acknowledge that I am loved and supported by the forces governing my universe, and I am a conduit of this love and support for myself and for others. I choose to love myself fully, to accept my past as part of my divine journey, and to forgive, appreciate, and embrace all the people, places, and things in my life as my access to that divine love. I orient myself now to my truth, my power, and my love within, and I author my life in a co-creative way that serves my highest good as well as the highest good of all those around me, free from any and all fears or doubts. I am my most authentic self, and I express myself fully as such to create a life I love. And so, it is.

"EVERY
ACCOMPLISHMENT
STARTS WITH
THE DECISION
TO TRY."

— JFK

CHAPTER 24

FLY DADDY BIRD, FLY

There I was, sitting on the front pew of a Southern Baptist church, not sure what I was going to say, or how I was going to say it.

The words from Dionne Warwick's, "That's What Friends Are For," began playing in my mind.

"Keep smiling, keep shining, knowing you can always count on me...for sure..."

Except in this version, it didn't end with, "That's what friends are for."

My mind ended it with, "That's what fags are for."

I wondered what the pastor would think if he knew.

I mean, it totally makes sense that I'd be singing this song in my head at a Baptist church.

Honestly, I'm surprised it's not already Hymn #112, just in between, "Holy Holy Holy," and "Just as I am."

In any event, remember in the preface how I was at a Baptist church for my son's choir rehearsal, but the only time you'd usually see me there would be for a wedding or a funeral?

Well that day was my father's memorial.

He had just lost his five-month battle with brain cancer, and there I sat, singing a fag song in my mind.

In true, "Marine meets Southern Baptist pastor" fashion, dad's former self would have been riddled with shock and awe over my current mental state.

His new self, however, was probably laughing hysterically, flying his fighter jet of unconditional love amongst the clouds.

Even though he had flown and crashed two F4's in his service to our country, cancer was what actually took his life, and he went from stroke to death in a matter of five months.

And before I got the call from my mom about his stroke, it had been almost a year and a half since he and I had spoken at my kitchen counter on the hot topic of homosexuality being the precursor to the downfall of society.

At the time, I chose to see that statement as a projection of his own judgment, to look on him with compassion and forgiveness, and to let go of any expectation that he be anyone other than who he was, while at the same time creating the boundary for myself that I could love him unconditionally as well as stop trying so hard to earn his approval.

For approval is never earned, it is received.

I decided that I was going to stop trying so hard — that I wasn't going to call and be so deliberate with a relationship — that if he wanted me in his life, he'd make an attempt to do so.

I thought that if I pulled back my efforts to communicate that he'd call or check in.

Nope.

A year's worth of birthdays and holidays for myself and for my children.

Nothing.

Part of me was hurt, and the greater part of me was relieved and thankful.

He had made his choice, and I got to move into a space of deeper love for myself as I approved of myself apart from attempting to earn or receive his earthly validation.

There was no dramatic downfall with us, just a slow fading away of that which was never a deep relationship anyway, AND it was all an opportunity for me to rely on and validate myself.

Which in and of itself, is the best gift that he could have ever given me.

As time went on, I continued to practice love and forgiveness, knowing that dad was just dad, and that his mental illness, PTSD, and whatever else kept him from expressing himself to me was just what was so.

Until the day where his brain conked out, and I chose that it didn't matter if he thought I was the precursor to the downfall of society, it mattered MORE that I considered myself a precursor not to the downfall, but to the UPLIFTING of the world.

A phone call was just a phone call.

A conversation was just a conversation.

I had told myself that if he wanted to talk, he could call me.

But something about him having 20+ brain tumors required me to amend my communication boundaries.

So, before his surgery, I called.

Even though he wasn't really cognizant of what I was saying, I told him that I loved him.

He cried (something he never did) and talked about how he thought Jesus was going to take him on the operating table.

He ended up making it through the surgery, and then on Father's Day, even though he didn't speak back or respond, I called again to tell him that I was proud of him.

Shortly before he passed, I told him that I knew he did his best, there was strength in weakness, and it was okay to let go.

What a journey, right?!

So back to me singing fag songs in a church pew.

That weekend, my mother had been slightly (and by, 'slightly,' I mean, 'almost completely') neurotic about the funeral plans, and making sure my father, "Ended well," as she liked to say about 999 times a day.

And ending well meant that my brother and I were to share "the best things and memories about dad."

Sidebar, what is it about dying that erases all our sins?

Certainly, I did not want to trash talk my father, but my call to authenticity does NOT include sugar coating how life shows up either.

"So, what WAS this fag for, right here and now?" I thought to myself as I pondered what I was going to say.

Most people have a plan on what they're going to say before they speak publicly, but usually I choose to go with the flow and allow Divinity to show up in the moment.

Nine times out of ten it's scary as hell, and ten times out of ten it's totally worth it.

It wasn't until my brother shared right before me that I felt lead to share what I did, and my clarity was revealed.

He read a, "Dear Dad" letter that he had written.

It was heartfelt and genuine, and it opened me up to the possibility that honoring our father wasn't about erasing what we thought were his sins, but that honoring him was about acknowledging and being grateful for the good.

That morning I had posted a, "Dear Dad" letter to Facebook, and even though it wasn't all the rainbows and sunshine that my mother would have liked, after my brother read his letter, I knew I had to read mine as well.

Part of it basically had me coming out too, as I referred to myself a "weird kid who played with stickers and ribbons" growing up, even though my fighter-jet-flying colonel of a dad probably wanted to talk about tactical air strike maneuvers.

Before I went up to share, I thought, “Well, it looks like these church folks are gonna give me the floor, so I better twirl it up nice for ‘em!”

Because when I read the line about playing with stickers and ribbons, I added a few extra S’s to make it clear that I was slightly more than just a ‘weird’ kid.

Leave it to me to be “extra” at my dad’s Baptist funeral.

It had been years since I worked through the anger, hurt, and rejection that the church had projected onto me for being who I was, so I was not uncomfortable there.

In fact, it was the years of work that allowed my ease in being there.

To know that my message of authenticity, acceptance, forgiveness and unconditional love for ALL of our life experience is a universal one.

A message that transcends any building.

We ALL want these things.

So, I shared my heart right there standing on that blue-green carpet next to that old-fashioned stained-glass window.

Old wooden pews...soft human hearts.

A place I never would have thought I’d be when I first began this book.

Such a deep space of forgiveness for my father, for myself, and for God.

And a space of an even deeper unconditional love for all of it.

His perceived rejection, a gift of access to connection.

His perceived harshness, a gift of access to gentleness.

And his perceived judgment, a gift of access to an unconditionally loving God.

My human dad, with all his faults, led me to the unconditional love that is my heaven within.

I am pretty sure that you don't clap at a funeral, but at the end of my share, the attendees gave me a round of applause.

And I knew that dad...the REAL, hysterically laughing dad... was there.

The approval of the audience, which was completely irrelevant about whether or not I received, reflected my own approval, and a willingness to share from my heart about what authenticity and forgiveness meant to me.

At the reception a veteran friend of my dad came up to me and thanked me.

With tear-soaked eyes he showed me a picture of one of his six grown children...a daughter who had cut him out of her life.

He told me that one day he wished his daughter could forgive him the way I had forgiven my father.

It was one of the most moving moments of my life.

And it was in that moment that I knew even more what my life was for.

Not just to share the message of love and forgiveness, but to love every damn step along the way, and hope that you will too.

Each person, place, and thing are access to love right where we are.

No place to go.

No person to get to.

No final destination point at which we will arrive.

We are here just to love.

The steppingstones along the river.

The hippity hops along the path.

And all the big leaps in between.

It was all for love.

Just what THIS FAG was for.

IS for.

My father's death...

Now my rebirth.

His burial...

Now my resurrection.

His ending...

Now my beginning.

So, with that I'll say, "Fly daddy bird, fly, I'll meet you in the clouds. And any time I can't see you, I'll just follow the laughter in my heart and yours, for now we are both completely free to love, on earth as it is in heaven."

So shall it be, and so it is.

Thank you, thank you, thank you.

Amen.

Mahalo.

Aho.

GIFT 24:
EMBRACE YOUR CRUCIFIXION AS ACCESS TO YOUR RESURRECTION

You know I needed to share the religious connotation until the end -- consider it my alter call, ha-ha. I do hope that if you've suffered from any kind of religious PTSD as I have, that you've gotten some solace from my story, and even gotten the relief you seek by doing the work I've suggested. Personally, I feel that most of the Bible is a metaphor -- the hints are that Christ spoke mainly in parables. And also, it started off with a talking snake! My point is that life is supposed to be a mystery. We're not supposed to have everything mapped out for us, nor are we born with manuals like robots. The joy is in the mystery. Love is found in the rapture of not knowing where you're going but trusting the Source anyway.

And Christ gave us some really amazing examples of that. I personally believe that we're living his second coming. Our awakening is the resurrection. And we must experience our own figurative death to bring about this resurrection. We can be crucified in any number of ways, to include crucifying ourselves most days. But the point of the process is to acknowledge that those hurts, those pains, all of it, you can allow to give you access to freedom. Your freedom. Your resurrection.

Forgive them, for they know not what they do.

Let that sink in for everyone you know.

Let that sink in for yourself.

Let them all off the hook of expecting them to be anyone other than who they are, then give YOURSELF this same grace and understanding.

You've been crucifying yourself for years, so now is the time to resurrect YOURSELF.

APPLICATION

Ask yourself, are there areas in your life where you are holding on to a belief that says you still need to suffer and/ or pay the price for something you did?

How would your life go if you held on to this way of being and continued your current course of actions?

What do you see happening if you chose to rewrite a new story?

INSPIRED ACTION:

Well I've asked you to dance, make amends, meditate, burn stuff, send cards, make lists, and twenty-something other things in between.

So today is up to you.

Make something up. Or do something again that you already did. You're the boss of your life. Consider yourself graduated from this book and do whatever practice you feel will enable your resurrection. The key is to be in an action that reinforces this as a reality for you. Trust yourself. You are good. What you want is good. We've got this... together.

After you have completed the action, take three deep breaths and repeat this phrase:

I accept the sacred orientation that is my knowing deep down. I acknowledge that I am loved and supported by the forces governing my universe, and I am a conduit of this love and support for myself and for others. I choose to love myself fully, to accept my past as part of my divine journey, and to forgive, appreciate, and embrace all the people, places, and things in my life as my access to that divine love. I orient myself now to my truth, my power, and my love within, and I author my life in a co-creative way that serves my highest good as well as the highest good of all those around me, free from any and all fears or doubts. I am my most authentic self, and I express myself fully as such to create a life I love. And so, it is.

CONCLUSION

Well congratulations, you made it, you little authenticity junkie you!

Thank you so much for taking this journey with me. I hope you've gotten to know me a bit more, but more importantly I hope you've gotten to know yourself more -- and to love yourself more as a result. To love yourself SO MUCH that you bring your FULL self-expression to the world.

That you show us all just how beautiful and loving you are.

That you forgive others and yourself.

That you get YOUR MESSAGE out to the world.

That you stand up for what you believe, even if it just means taking one step.

It took me SO LONG to actually get this done.

I had leaked the stories out via Facebook posts close to two years ago.

I wasn't sure what the book or stories were going to look like, just that I HAD to share what I shared...so, I shared them.

And then I started trying to compile them and make a package out of it.

And then I got stopped.

By the very messages I am seeking to overcome with this book! Oh, the irony.

Stories/memes like, “Who am I to do this, I have no authority on this, I’m no expert, I have to have a bigger platform” went on and on in my head.

I even considered opening a restaurant first, as a means to “give myself a platform” from which to speak!

What I got out of the whole delay was that I already had a platform. I am the platform. I’ve done enough. And my declaration of such is ENOUGH!

I took my own damn medicine I was writing.

In truth though, I didn’t write this book, this book wrote me.

I am so grateful for you reading it and I hope to do many, many more.

Please remember that you came from love. You’ll return to love. You have nothing to give but love. And you have nothing to receive but love.

It’s all love.

I love you.

I thank you.

And I appreciate you.

Until next time,

~~ Case